FROM THE GUTTERMOST TO THE UTTERMOST

Apostle Winston G. Baker

From The Guttermost to The Uttermost
Copyright ©2023 Winston G. Baker

ISBN 978-1506-911-16-8 PBK
ISBN 978-1506-911-17-5 EBK

September 2023

Published and Distributed by
First Edition Design Publishing, Inc.
P.O. Box 17646, Sarasota, FL 34276-3217
www.firsteditiondesignpublishing.com

All scriptures quoted are from the King James Version of the Holy Bible.

Contents

*And we know that all things work together for
good to them that love God, to them who are
the called according to His purpose.*
Romans 8:28

Introduction

Since the day I set out in obedience to the Spirit of God to write, I entered a new realm of spiritual warfare. Immediately after my first book, 'WARRING UNCLEAN SPIRITS' was launched, from numerous reports, it was clear that the attacks were extended to my reading audience.

However, through the power of the blood of Jesus Christ, we prevailed! Readers militantly engaged the enemy in warfare as they read and followed the instructions God gave in that tool. Numerous testimonies are being received, heralding the victories which God's people have been experiencing.

The Almighty God has faithfully led me to release a second book, 'THE LEADER WHO COVERS' a third book, 'THE KINGDOM MANDATE HANDBOOK' and a fourth book, the one you are reading at this moment.

Spiraling interest in the prior publications is indicative of the fact that the readers are tenacious and relentless. There is a strong determination that nothing will deter them from unearthing the life-transforming messages enveloped in each release.

As an Ambassador for Christ and a warrior, I release the story of my exodus, 'FROM THE GUTTERMOST TO THE UTTERMOST' with this prayer:

Father, in the name of Jesus, here I am through Your blood;

Father, please, let the blood saturate the spot of ground which Your people occupy right now. Permeate the atmosphere with Your blood, pulling down every stronghold.

Let Your blood touch the minds of Your people.

I come against every attacking force right now! I render them powerless by the precious blood of Jesus Christ.

Father, I thank You in Jesus' name.

Let God arise and His enemies be scattered! Please Holy Spirit, loose high-ranking angels. Give them swords of flaming fire! Let them burn unclean spirits; Let the Holy Ghost have its way!

Sit upon Your people; loose them Oh Lord God Almighty, as this message is released. Do what You love to do: loose, deliver, save, and fill with Your Holy Ghost and fire. Oh God, heal and set somebody free through Your blood.

Let Apostolic grace sit upon Your people. Every trap and every plot that the enemy has set, we nullify in the name of Jesus. Destroy that plan in the name of Jesus. Satan, we render you powerless! It shall not be so by the power of Jesus' name.

Father, I thank You! In Jesus name

Amen

Clap your hands and begin to shout, 'The blood of Jesus!'

The blood of Jesus!

The blood of Jesus!

Hallelujah!

Clap your hands and give the Lord God Almighty, the honour, the glory and the praise.

PART 1

THE GUTTERMOST

Chapter 1

Winner From The Womb

Before the foundation of the world, I was a thought in the mind of God. When the fullness of time came, David Baker and Sylvia Rhoden came together and produced their last child by the process of human fertilization. This process involved the union of an egg from Sylvia with sperm from David. The union resulted in the production of a fertilized egg and my prenatal development began.

I did a little study and discovered that the average volume of semen in a human ejaculation range from two to six millilitres. I have also been informed that a man releases two hundred to five hundred million sperm in each ejaculation. The details of how many millions of sperm competed with me on the day of my conception are irrelevant at this point. The notable fact here is that, I, Winston George Baker-also known as Donovan-won the race!

Here I am today, a winner from the womb! Glory to God!

My mother had already given birth to Steve, Faye, Sonia, Rollie and Richie, but I had to get here. My father already produced the latter three children as well as Violet, Charles, Linda, Joycie and Pat from two previous relationships. But I had to get here! God foreknew me and according to Romans 8:29-30:

> *Whom He did foreknow, He also did predestinate to be conformed to the image of His Son, that He might be the firstborn among many brethren.*
>
> *Moreover, whom He did predestinate, them He also called: and whom He called, them He also justified; and whom He justified, them He also glorified.*

As the various stages of my life unfolded, it confirmed that I was not an afterthought of God. Initially, I struggled to believe it, as I was the last and least among my brethren. Fortunately, or unfortunately, I could not change anything. God had placed me in that family, at the time He did.

Double runs in my family on both sides. My mother, who was affectionately called Martha, had a twin sister called Mary. My father's father, whose name was Jacob, also had a twin brother named Esau. Well, except for the fact that my mother, father and grandfather were all named after Bible characters, I am yet to establish any other significance to this occurrence.

My first dwelling after leaving the Savanna-la-mar Public General Hospital was Cooke Street, Savanna-la-mar in the parish of Westmoreland. There, I lived with my other siblings, except for my eldest brother Steve and my sister Sonia. Steve resided with his father's grandmother in Little London, where he was also schooled. At three years, Sonia had gone to live with my father's parents, Jacob and Matilda Baker.

This extended family also included Miss Iris Bowens and my father's first two children, whom she mothered. Their dwelling place was 11 Segree Street in Savanna-la-mar, Westmoreland.

Mother did domestic work most of her life. She also worked as an ancillary worker at Hammond's Bakery in my hometown for many years. My father David Baker was a 'Jack of all trades' and an only child for both parents. His parents left no stone unturned to ensure he maximized his true potential.

He served in the Jamaica Constabulary Force as a special constable for most of his adult life. However, this did not deter him from developing his musical skills. Indeed, he was multitalented! He played the drum, banjo, guitar and flute. Eventually, he established his own band and both played and taught music. Oh! I almost forgot to tell you that he was also a tailor.

The early years of my childhood were quite normal. Sister Faye, being the eldest daughter of my mother, was left with the responsibility of caregiver for her younger siblings.

My sister Faye often saw the need to scold me for misbehaving. I recall her reminding me that on one of those occasions, my mother said to her, "Yuh tan deh a beat him. Him ago preach a yuh funeral." Mama told her that when I was only five years old, I woke up one morning and told her that an angel had visited me and told me that I was going to be a great preacher.

I told you that I was predestined!

Later we relocated to Dalling Street in the same town of Savanna-la-mar. At thirteen, my sister Faye went to live with her father and I was left with my sister Rollie, my brother Ritchie and Mama.

I have no information about my mother's parents. However, I am aware that my father's folks were ardent members of the Methodist Church. Unfortunately, they all died before I got the privilege to get acquainted with them.

Mama did all she possibly could for us with her meagre resources. She migrated to the United States of America in the year 2000. There she resided with my sister Sonia, who migrated when I was seventeen.

Mama vacationed here in Jamaica yearly. However, strangely, in November 2010 she came on her usual vacation and insisted on not going back to America. At her request, Sister Sonia extended her stay. Immediately after, God granted her request and on February 8, 2011, she slept into eternity. Mama was and will remain dear to my heart.

This was an emotionally challenging time for me, but God provided much-needed comfort as our family laid her to rest. At the point of her death, she was processing documents for me to migrate to the United States of America. Her death delayed that process and Sister Sonia decided to continue. It has been several years and I am still in Jamaica. Although I have been to the United States of America on business for the King and His kingdom, I believe He blocked my migration as I have His work to do here.

The main purpose for chronicling my experiences is to reveal how God orders the steps of His children. While much of it leaves me emotional, I constantly see the mighty hand of God on my life in everything that I have done and continue to do.

At the age of eight, I arrived at 11 Segree Street and was embraced by two of the most loving and caring arms which have ever held me. They were the angelic arms of Miss Iris Bowens. Her untainted love towards me blew my mind and exceeded all my expectations. I must confess, she spoiled me!

She was a woman of God! An ardent member of the Holiness Born Again Apostolic Church on Barclay's Street. Undoubtedly, this was a divine encounter. Who would imagine that years later, this was the same place where I took on the name of Jesus in water baptism too?

In retrospect, I think that like Moses' mother, she had discerned that I was a 'goodly child'. She discerned that I was predestinated for a special work in the kingdom of God. Her placement in my life at such a tender age nurtured that which God had hidden within me.

In addition to Sonia and me, Miss Iris added Rollie to her extended family, leaving Ritchie alone with Mama. Miss Iris took me to church and she prayed without ceasing. During her final years, she grew feeble and could no longer make the journey to Barclay's Street. This did not hinder her from being in God's house. This little "Jesus lover" instead began worshipping at the Wesleyan Holiness Church next door to us. She remained faithful until she went to be with the Lord.

This was all part of God's master plan for my life.

The Church of Christ became my next religious ground. I accompanied my sisters there when Miss Iris became a shut-in. They both got baptized, along with the other members of our extended family.

Shortly afterwards, except for Sister Rollie, they all backslid. Rollie loved the Lord and was very faithful to Him. She was quite active and served as a Sunday School teacher. My God! Her passion for the things of God and education was astounding. She was always studying her Bible.

Regrettably, she was a gift that I did not appreciate until long after she was gone. You can imagine that her disposition made her very strict. Her insistence that I adhere to her rules, like regularly attending church and maintaining high academic performance in school, was quite overbearing. Of course, I interpreted her actions as the recipe to deprive me of a happy childhood. I despised her for that.

Unknown to me, she was nurturing greatness and before I could blossom, she was gone. The cruel hands of death crept in and used the wicked tool of bone cancer to steal her from us.

It all happened so fast. At nineteen, she began to complain that she was feeling pain. On her first visit to the doctor, she received antibiotics and pain relievers. However, the pains did not subside, so she was taken to the Savanna-la-mar Hospital, where she was admitted. Stronger medications were administered, yet her condition worsened. Finally, a series of testing diagnosed her with bone cancer.

Within a year, Sister Rollie was no longer with us. Her untimely death sent emotional shockwaves through the family. She was so young; so beautiful; so promising and so full of life.

Although it was a very difficult time for the family, I must admit that I felt somewhat relieved that she would not be around to 'pressure' me anymore. Sonia and Rollie always acted like mothers to me. Rollie was sometimes unable to attend school in order to stay home with me.

I would not consider myself to have been a rude child. At least, Miss Iris saw to that. She ensured that I did absolutely nothing. I mean nothing at all! At all! At all! Chores were no exemptions, much to the displeasure of my family members.

Until today, I am occasionally reminded of how much Miss Iris spoiled me. "Everybody got chores except her favourite, Donovan," I would hear. Whatever was assigned for me to do, she would go right ahead and do it herself. Even when I was grown, she continued to set my warm bath and soap my rag.

Anyone who dared to discipline me would have to attempt it at the expense of a head-on collision with Miss Iris' fury. She would 'let them have it!'

Albeit she planted Godly seeds which were watered by others; religiously, every night before I was granted the privilege of retiring to bed, I had to kneel at Miss Iris' bedside and pray. She would say to me, "You are not coming up in this bed until you pray." Since then, I have learnt that prayer is the key to accessing so much more than Miss Iris' bed.

Sadly, Miss Iris exited this life the year following my Sister Rollie's painful death. However, this was not before making an indelible mark on my life. So, by the age of thirteen, I had witnessed the death of two very important figures in my life. What a time to lose loved ones and especially those who truly care! Right on the verge of my turbulent teen years, I was without the hands that held me in place and gave me affection and direction.

My life was changed forever! But, as you will eventually realize, God was still in total control. He is an immutable God! And despite all the things which were about to follow, His plan and purpose for my life would still be fulfilled. I am predestined!

I always had a passion for dancing; it feels innate. I could make all the moves of Michael Jackson and perfected the moonwalk. When the popular television programme 'Top Ten and Twenty' was being broadcast on Friday nights, I would dance like crazy. Before long, no one was watching the television. Instead, all eyes were glued on me. To this point, life was fairly normal.

Chapter 2

Obscurity

Ah! Life happened and I flowed with it. I entered my teenage years under somewhat new management. Sister Sonia, at twenty-three, now had full responsibility for me. I simply refused to listen to her! After all, this was the first time I was experiencing 'freedom'. There was no more sister Rollie to "pressure" me. I was free to do whatever I wanted to do, whenever I wanted to do it. I'm sorry but sister Sonia was not going to stand in my way. I was ready to explore and conquer.

Despite her insistence, I refused to stay in the house. However, not being disrespectful, I waited for her to fall asleep before making my move. This was accomplished by removing the window panes at the back of the house. I quickly ran my little errands and came back inside before she discovered that I was missing.

Fortunately for me, sister Sonia began dating. Do you know what that means? She had other priorities now too. Not surprisingly, within a year she was expecting her first and only child, Renee.

Soon after her daughter was born, I was on the move again. Sister Sonia sent me to live with my father and his wife at their home at 17 Rose Street, in Savanna-la-mar.

She decided to relocate to Hanover where Renee's father resided. She soon returned to 11 Segree Street and eventually migrated to the United States of America. However, I remained at Rose Street until I was nineteen.

Chapter 3

Popularity

I was always influential! I just did not realize it. Whatever I loved, I committed myself to perfecting. I did it with all my heart and made sure I was the best I could be, especially in football and dancing. To say that I was passionate about them is an understatement.

I recall playing for at least ten different football teams in different seasons. Believe it or not, I was totally committed to each team at the time I played for them. Each team considered my skillfulness, instead of focusing on the fact that I had previously played for a rival team. They just needed me on their team! This sport earned me some amount of popularity.

Eventually, my interest in dancing took precedence over my interest in football. My passion for perfection played a pivotal role in how quickly I rose to prominence as a dancer in western Jamaica. Along with friends, the 'Fresh Boyz Dance Group' was formed.

Again, I became very skillful in this arena and led the group to win several gold awards. This includes being five-time gold medalists at the national finals of Jamaica Cultural Development Commission - JCDC.

Chapter 4

The Call

'New level, new devil' is a common expression which unfolds in the life of anyone called to full-time ministry. I am no exemption! Firstly, the zeal of God consumes the very fibre of my being. Most people cannot understand my reason for being so passionate about the things of God. The driving force behind what I do is unfathomable and I am often misunderstood.

I accepted Jesus as my personal Lord and Saviour, on October 26, 1996. I remember the details as if it happened only yesterday. My dance group had danced at a hotel the night before and early the next morning Alcapone (now Overseer Terrance Mullings) and Shabba left me at the hotel. It was the first and last time that they ever left me after a performance.

While they were gone, I decided to find a nice movie to watch on HBO. I was switching through channels to get to HBO, when I heard a man saying "Try Jesus!" When I heard it, I stopped and said to myself, "Try Jesus?" My understanding of trying Jesus at the time was to go to the bathroom, lift my hands and say 'Jesus!' and see what happens.

I finally found and began watching a horror movie on HBO. While watching the movie, I heard a voice saying, "Try Jesus! Try Jesus! Try Jesus!" I responded to the voice in my heart. I told it that when the movie finishes, I will 'try Jesus'. The movie finished and I heard the voice again, "Try Jesus! Try Jesus! Try Jesus!"

I opened my mouth and said, "When I get to Sea Castle, I will try Jesus." This was the next hotel we were scheduled to perform. The voice responded, "What's so hard in trying Jesus?" After reasoning with the voice, I agreed that of a truth, it shouldn't be so hard to try Jesus.

I got up, went to the bathroom, lifted both hands and shouted "Jesus! Jesus! If you are real, I want to know!" I then shouted 'Jesus!' four more times and at the fourth shout, I saw a light brighter than the sun entered through the roof of the bathroom.

The light hit me on both knees. Somebody was talking to me, but I did not hear what the person was saying. However, I was certain that somebody was there. As the voice spoke in my spirit, I heard myself responding, "Yes Jesus! Yes Jesus! Yes Jesus!" I never understood what was really happening.

My eyes opened and I found myself shivering profusely and I was soaking wet. Suddenly, there was a knock at the door. I proceeded towards the door, which was unlocked. It was Andre, our chaperone. He was responsible for giving us props and anything else that we needed to enhance our dance routines.

"What's wrong with you?" he asked. "Mi nuh know!" was my response. Tears were heavily streaming down my face. In between sobs, I explained that I had only gone into the bathroom, shouted Jesus, was hit by a bright light, fell on my knees and started to cry and shiver uncontrollably.

"I know what is taking place with you", Andre admitted. "I am a backslider, so I can relate. I was baptized in the name of Jesus Christ for the remission of sins and I received the gift of the Holy Ghost. What is taking place in your life is a visitation from God. It is God calling you. You need to find a church that does baptism in Jesus' name for the remission of sins."

Andre needed to say no more. Immediately, I decided that I was going to get baptized and change my life. Nothing could stop me! Without hesitation, I got on the phone and called my sister Faye.

"Faye, guess what just happened to me?" I rhetorically asked. Before long, I proceeded to share my testimony with her. She was of the Jehovah's Witness faith and didn't really understand what was taking place. With much concern in her voice, she said, "Donovan, remember dancing a yuh work enuh. Anyways, if that's how you feel, dance one more time and den stop."

Relieved, I got on a bus headed for Sea Castle Hotel and checked in. When I got there, to my surprise, Alcapone and Shabba had not yet arrived. The moment I checked into our room, I saw a Gideon Bible staring me in the eyes. I opened it and began what I call 'counting words', as at the time I could hardly read.

Shortly after, they came and saw me reading the Bible. Shabba burst out in laughter and said, "Baker! Baker, yuh tun Christian!"

The routine we were to do that night was called 'Mock the Christian'. It required that one dancer pretended to be a pastor. Preaching would be played, and the pastor would mimic the preaching. The other two dancers would pretend to be Christians who were moving in the power of the Holy Ghost.

That night, as the routine began, the dancehall songs played, followed by the preaching and we began our act. I was one of the dancers who should pretend to get into Spirit. But instead of me getting into the Spirit, the Spirit got into me. I bawled!

The following day, I did not go to the next hotel for which we were scheduled. Instead, I headed straight home. As soon as I got home, I looked at my child's mother and said, "Hear wha happen now, God touch mi an seh mi need fi change mi life an serve Him."

We had met a few years prior, after one of my performances. We lived together for a while and then we had our first son, Romario. In my discussions with her, I reassured her that I would continue to take care of my son. However, I would be moving from the house we shared to go back to my father's house.

Recall, Andre advised me to find a church that does baptism in Jesus' name. I did! That Sunday, I attended the Holiness Born Again Apostolic Church on Barclay's Street. This was the same church to which Miss Iris took me as a little boy.

That Sunday night, at the end of the service, I walked to the altar and told them that I was ready to serve God. They said, "OKAY!" From the altar, I was taken to the pool. There, I was interrogated about my personal life. I disclosed that I was presently living with my child's mother, but I had made plans to return to my father's house.

"Have you spoken with her about your decision?" I was then asked. Once more, I said, 'Yes." Again, I reiterated my decision to change my life and continue maintaining my son.

To my dismay, the baptizer responded, "Well, you can't baptize as yet, because if you get baptized, the child's mother is going to give you problem." I was devastated. I walked out with tears in my eyes.

Determined, I went back the following Sunday. Again, an altar call was made, and they asked who wanted to be baptized. My hands quickly went up once more. This time, I changed into the baptismal clothes and was happy that I was about to be baptized.

The baptizer looked at me, as before, and asked, "Didn't I talk to you?" I agreed that we spoke a week ago. I told him that I had gone back to my son's mother and discussed the way forward again. We are both comfortable with the arrangement, I tried to persuade the baptizer. She is in total agreement with me getting baptized. However, he was not convinced. He just wanted to confirm whether I got married. I still had not got married, so I said, "No."

I was further devastated when I realized they were adamant that I needed to be married before I got baptized. I relented, got married and was then baptized. This experience has taught me a lot. Most importantly, souls are more important than anything else in this world.

While I greatly honour and admire this leader, this practice is not upheld in my Ministry. If someone desires to be baptized, I perform the baptism. Who knows, the day someone requests to be baptized and have their sins remitted could be their last day on earth. According to John 3:5, *Except a man be born of water and of the Spirit, he cannot enter into the kingdom of God.* I would not want anyone to be denied the most important opportunity by refusing them water baptism.

Despite my experience, I was excited to now be a part of the family of God. One month and fifteen days after being baptized in water, I received the baptism of the Holy Ghost with the evidence of speaking in unknown tongues.

One year and nine months later, I was called to exhort for the very first time. In retrospect, being shy and not the least bit eloquent, I must have done a poor job. Guess what? I was never called upon again until one year later.

During this period of silence in the church, I constantly shared the good news in the byways and hedges. It never bothered me that I was not allowed to minister in the local congregation. Some made a mockery of my ministry because I would pray for the people along the roadways and without fear, allowed God to use me to cast out unclean spirits.

It was reported that a prominent church leader asked sarcastically, "Can a man pump demon out of a wall?" Until this very moment, I burst into laughter at the remembrance of that utterance. They had no idea what God was doing in and through me at all! At all! At all!

A young minister whose conversion came through my outreach ministry was called to exhort after he became a member of the church. He was a great blessing to the congregation. Seemingly, this prompted my being asked to exhort the following week. The leader had discovered that I was the one who was mentoring him.

I realized immediately that God was doing me a favour during the period that I was not asked to speak publicly in the church. To say I was nervous is an understatement. I studied all week! I fasted and prayed without ceasing!

The night finally came, and I did what I continue to do today. Each time I face a crowd, I surrender all that I am to Jesus so that He can use all that I am to bring Him glory. I humbly report to you that two persons were filled with the Holy Ghost during my ministry. I am not sure what the leaders saw from where they stood. From that night, I was regularly called upon to preach the word of God. And preach I did!

Recently, one of my sons asked, "Daddy, how come you never get up in any congregation to bring greetings?" My answer was simple, "Son, I can only do what I am anointed to do - preach." And that is true in every sense of the word. The boldness that comes to me as I stand before any congregation is simply to preach God's undiluted truth.

In obedience to the Spirit of God, I was anointed with oil from the pulpit of my birthplace in Christ. Praise God for Godly men and women who can recognize and nurture the gifts of God in young believers. Not many can do so without envy, jealousy or covetousness.

Thank God that I was never paid to preach. As a result, very early these principles from the Holy Scriptures were engraved within my spirit:

Freely ye have received, freely give.

To God be the glory, I was never reluctant to preach. Being hungry for physical food, I ate the word and preached it every opportunity I got. The bread of life is to be broken for the nourishment of God's people, whether we are empty or full.

Many people who speak of hunger are speaking of a situation in which what they desire to eat is not available and as a result of that they have not eaten. When I speak of hunger, I am referring to being so hungry that my stomach and my intestines writhe in pain. When I speak of hunger, I am referring to being so starved that when I attempted to spit, there was absolutely no saliva. Yet I am in total agreement with Paul when he says:

I can do all things through Christ which strengtheneth me.

Glory be to God! I still preached even when the person receiving a word of blessing from the Lord through me is an outright enemy. Who am I to decide that I will not release the word of blessing? It matters not that God has decided to bless someone who has cursed me.

I know that people who speak evil of me behind my back at times come to me for prayers. At their request, I lay my hand and pray as the Spirit of God gives utterance. Sometimes they walk away, confessing that I am a real man of God. Jesus is my example, so I follow hard after Him.

While answering the call, I do not allow my emotions to be swayed by the accolades of men. Not surprisingly, they will do to me as they did to Jesus. Mankind will say, "Hosanna!" today and "Crucify him!" tomorrow. But preach I must. I answered the call and must fulfil God's command.

Thank God I preach even when known witchcraft workers attend my meetings. Some are there believing that they have the power to intimidate and shut me up from preaching and delivering those who are bound. Others are there because they got into deep trouble because of unclean spirits which others have assigned to destroy them.

The latter not only comes for prayer but surrenders to Jesus Christ and enters into a covenant with Him through water baptism. Regardless, I echo the message without apology. Acts 2:38 admonishes us to repent and be baptized in Jesus' name. Those who reject the message leave and gather reinforcement to take my life. But preach I must! Man did not call me! Man did not hire me! Man cannot fire me!

The things that I experience in life before answering the call to ministry have all proved useful in shaping me. They inform how I father the flock which God has entrusted to my care. Persons, including officers and other church leaders, are sometimes very critical of my leadership style. This is my response: I learnt from the way my Father - Jesus- treats me. I must be merciful because I have and continue to obtain more mercy than I ever dreamed of.

Chapter 5
Rejection

The Fresh Boyz dance group which I led, won a gold medal at the Jamaica Cultural Development Commission (JCDC) annual competitions for the fifth consecutive time. Soon, I plummeted to the pinnacle of my dancing career. Celebrations were quite in order! But destiny had other plans.

My jubilance was short-lived by a Joseph-like moment. Except that -unlike me- Joseph was completely innocent of touching Potiphar's wife. A female with whom I had a mutual intimate moment showed up at my home with her mother and police officers, nine months after our encounter.

Everyone looked curiously and waited to hear the reason for their visit. My world collapsed within a split second after she pointed me out to the police. They laid hands on me and took me to jail where I was facing fifteen years of prison time.

A conspiracy to collect money from me led to my being accused of raping her at gunpoint, nine months prior. She claimed to have run naked from my house to hers. At the time, the mere shock that someone could have concocted such a lie was enough to destroy me emotionally.

A barrage of negative emotions enveloped my wounded soul. How could anyone be so cruel to watch someone's life being utterly ruined, without showing any remorse? It was over for me! Or so I thought! But God had it all in control. I just did not know it.

My life became a living hell. I thought I was having a nightmare and that I would wake up and realize that it had just been a bad dream. But, no! It was not a dream at all! At all! At all! It was a reality! My reality! I was literally scared to death!

Forgotten, like David in the cave; there were only a few persons who had not given up on me. Despite my predicament, they still believed that greatness was in me and they stood with me throughout this rather trying time.

One such person was Pastor and Evangelist Cynthia Myrie. She became an active part of my life shortly after I surrendered my life to Jesus Christ. She knew of me as a dancer and had somehow recognized the transformation in my life. Her entrance into my life was through a divine connection which remains intact.

During the legal battle, Pastor Myrie accompanied me to court. She constantly provided moral and spiritual support. She was indeed a woman of prayer, who continued to believe in me when others stopped.

I have faced many seasons of rejection in my life and have learnt several lessons from each experience. The greatest and most painful experiences have been the rejection by my immediate and church family. Those leave scars that time alone cannot heal. You heard me correctly, 'time alone CANNOT heal!' The wounds from these kinds of rejections could lead to chaos, deep depression, and even suicide.

Another low point in my life was when the mother of my four children, whom I had married, walked out on us. This resulted from constant disagreements and arguments between us. I was shattered and later fell from grace. I became the scorn of church folks. As if that were not enough, I was forced to resign from my job. My employers concluded that it was best for me to go home and take care of my children.

I struggled to make ends meet. Dancing was the only thing I knew. I had no qualifications and no trade. Anything my hand found to do, I attempted. Throwing mortar buckets on construction sites did not embarrass me. Neither did my entrepreneurial idea of riding on a bicycle selling icicles, ice-cream cakes and fudges.

Desperate times called for desperate measures. I had four little children I needed to provide for. The difficulty to make ends meet escalated to the point where I had to walk to my mother's home to secure a plate of food. This mile-and-a-half journey, I trod every night in desperation.

God bless her kind and loving heart. Her provision was supposed to be dinner for the children and me. I was faced with a major dilemma. If I ate my portion, the children would have to go without breakfast the following morning.

Whilst it was humanly difficult to bear the hunger, my love for them made the sacrifice easy. Hunger was my friend and the streets were somewhat a home. Hustling for my children became a priority.

I recall dancing one night in a deeply rural community. After performing, we were unable to access transportation to get home. Along with members of the dance group, a bus shed became our bed that night. It was cold out there! But I needed to feed my children.

There were times when everybody turned against me including my precious Sister Sonia. My loved ones grew frustrated with my lifestyle. Back then I was constantly getting into trouble and she always came to my rescue. In an effort to see if I would change, they pressured her to let me be.

It is a lonely walk! Many times, in the dark moments there is no one in this world to turn to for help. I have to confess that there were times when the enemy drove wedges between me and the very children of my loins. Through their rejection of a father who loved and cared for them as a single parent for many years, I discovered that I can only trust God. He alone never fails. I quickly learnt that if they can betray me, anyone else can.

It is only a test! 'It is only a test' were the words with which I comforted myself, as I watched my children grow and drifted away from me emotionally and physically.

Their mother had returned to the island after spending several years in the USA and they were yearning desperately to reestablish their mother-child bond. Their actions were sometimes in contradiction with my rules. Eventually, two of them left my home to live with her.

This would have been easier to accept if they were not rebelling against Christian principles. I watched them slowly but surely heading for destruction. The enemy threatened to steal, kill and destroy them! Then, like David, I cried to the Lord and He heard me and delivered me from my fears.

I learnt an important lesson in parenting during this heart-wrenching moment. The roles of each parent are equally essential to the total development of the children. In the absence of one parent, the other might try desperately to fill both roles. However, there is a void that can only be filled by a mother and another that can only be filled by a father. The damage done by the absence of any one parent can only be repaired by God.

The unfailing love of my children for their mother is nothing short of a demonstration of God's agape love. I thank God for His redemptive work in my life. The Lord will sometimes allow tragic circumstances, to prove our loyalty to Him. I remain committed to following Jesus, even if I have to do it alone! However, the mercies and love God showed me when I abandoned Him, made me realize what I needed to do for my straying children.

Daily, like the father of the Prodigal son, I looked out for them. My broken heart bled for them because for most of my life, they were all I had and I was all they had. One Father's Day, I sat on the rostrum, having just delivered a word from the Lord out of a broken spirit. Somehow, I was reduced to tears as I preached, being overwhelmed by a feeling of rejection. No one but God knew the horrible pain I was feeling inside. I find it difficult, if not impossible to look to "man" for help in desperate times. You see, I know where my help comes from.

King David said it like this in Psalm 121:

> *I will lift up mine eyes unto the hills, from whence cometh my help.*
>
> *My help cometh from the Lord, which made heaven and earth.*
>
> *He will not suffer thy foot to be moved: He that keepeth thee will not slumber.*
>
> *Behold, He that keepeth Israel shall neither slumber nor sleep.*
>
> *The Lord is thy keeper: the Lord is thy shade upon thy right hand.*
>
> *The sun shall not smite thee by day, nor the moon by night.*
>
> *The Lord shall preserve thee from all evil: He shall preserve thy soul.*
>
> *The Lord shall preserve thy going out and thy coming in from this time forth, and even for evermore.*

I was not spared, but through the comfort of the Holy Spirit and the redemptive power of Almighty God, I am an overcomer. God has anointed me to use my experiences, His word and the revelations He gives me positively. I have addressed the issue of rejection more extensively in my book, "Warring Unclean Spirits." In it, you can find powerful tools to gain victory over rejection. Thanks be to God, I did!

While I do not claim to be an expert on the causes of marriage and divorce, I will hasten to give this bit of advice. Ensure that your reason for entering into marriage is not simply to become a member of a church. Avoid this pitfall by prayerfully seeking God's will for your life, especially when seeking a marriage partner. You can be in love with someone who is not God's will for your life. It is very difficult to sever emotional bonds and soul ties, especially when young children are involved. However, it is better to obey God and remain single, if that is what will bring God glory. From experience, it is a great challenge; but we always say 'Better to be safe, than sorry'.

Of good note, is the fact that the Word of God referred to Eve as a "help meet" for Adam. Put another way, Eve was designed to support Adam in fulfilling His God-given mandate.

There is absolutely no doubt in my mind, that the valley experience was God's will. That is where God equipped me to father my children in the body of Christ today.

Chapter 6

I Never Lost My Praise

Simply put, it got rough, tough and rugged. Hunger was a close companion of mine. There were days when it was so severe, my mouth could not even produce saliva. My God! I remember feeling such horrible pain from being hungry that I rolled my pillow into a ball and curled around it to reduce the severity of the pain. But somehow, I never lost my praise!

Thank God for my sister Sonia! Despite the magnitude of her personal and family commitments in the United States of America and her obligations to Mama and Papa, she helped in whatever way she possibly could. From time to time help also came from members of my church family whom the Lord moved to bless us.

I will never forget those acts of kindness. I pause to pronounce a special blessing on the lives of all whom God used in various ways to provide much-needed assistance for us. God bless you all richly.

Praise God! I was called to the kingdom with a mandate to preach the message of the kingdom of God. I am a chosen vessel through which God transforms the lives of His people, both spiritually and physically.

My appreciation for the Salvation Army will never cease. My family was kept warm and clothed through their kindness towards us. This has been the driving force behind my zeal to ensure that the people of God have food to eat, a place to live and clothes to wear.

Can you imagine going home after church on a Sunday afternoon with four little children to collect sticks for a wood fire? In those days, kerosene oil was a luxury we could not afford. Our fires were lit using plastic bottles.

Can you further imagine your best Sunday meal being French fried chicken back and rice? Well, that was our reality! We consumed it gladly and were on our way back to church in no time. Our most prestigious mode of transportation was my famous colourless BMX bicycle. On it, the two younger children sat while the two older ones walked alongside it, holding on to my trousers. Glory to God! I never lost my praise!

I can recall some years ago I was at home with nothing to give the children. Times continued to be rough and hard but being a person who loves to pray, I was up praying one morning around 3:00 a.m. I cried, "God, please show up for me one more time." I prayed that until I fell asleep.

About 5:00 that morning, I heard a knocking at my door. I opened it and was greeted by Minister Marks (now an Elder). He said, "Bishop, I was home praying and the Lord told me to pack a bag and bring to you." Glory to God! When I checked he had brought me twenty-five pounds each of flour, sugar and rice. He had also brought canned food as well as other goodies. Tears came streaming down my face because Minister Marks lived in another parish, many miles away. He said that he was praying about 3:00 a.m. and I too, was praying about 3:00 a.m. He reached my house a little after 5:00 a.m.

So, the fact is that while I was making the request to God, He was working on Minister Marks' heart. After he gave me the food, he went into his pocket and said to me, "The Lord said to give you this." It was Three Thousand ($3000.00) Jamaican dollars.

My children were to go to school that morning and I didn't have lunch money to give to them but God showed up. I just want to tell somebody to keep trusting God. Continue to give Him praise because He never fails. He may not come when you want Him but He is always on time.

I can relate to a WhatsApp clip of a woman whom someone was trying to get to make her appeal to the public for help. Each time the camera was set for her to ask for help, she began bawling to God instead. In the video, she poured out her complaint to Father God. She kept on telling God that He is the only one who could help in her situation. This reminded me of myself! I can relate.

My family meant well, I am certain. A sure sign is their unwavering commitment to supporting me in everything I go through. My sister Linda was very rough on me whenever I lived my life loosely. However, in times of trouble, she was always there. Through it all, they remain a tower of strength until today in my ministry. For this, I am eternally grateful. May God reward their faithfulness!

Remember I said that one Father's Day I had just delivered a word from the Lord out of a broken spirit and was reduced to tears as I preached, being overwhelmed by a feeling of rejection. Well, this is an experience common among leaders which is usually not obvious to those they shepherd. It is common for leaders to be bleeding while they are leading. This was one of my moments but through it all, I continued to praise my Maker.

What God did next was indescribably amazing! The emotion-filled day of the father of the prodigal son as he returned home, became a reality for me. Delano, one of my sons who had gone to live with his mother, appeared out of nowhere, with tears streaming down his usually dry face. It appeared for a moment, that the devil was going to have the last laugh, but not before God swooped down and snatched him from his clutches.

Delano was never easily broken. He hardly ever cried and did an excellent job at hiding his emotions. That Father's Day, he walked straight to the rostrum and fell in my arms.

There was no space for air between us as we embraced each other. I could feel the transfer of untainted love between our hearts. It was as if he gave me his heart and I gave him mine. All that he had ever done to grieve me vanished and I was filled with unspeakable joy just knowing he was safe again.

The congregation rejoiced with me in that moment of victory. I can only imagine what went on in heaven as my lost son returned home. I praised God for having heard my cry.

Delano rededicated his life to the Lord and has been sold out to God since then. Unlike the previous years when he constantly rebelled against just about everything I stood for, we now share a similar passion for the ministry. In many ways, I now see myself in my children as their love for souls and the things of God consume them, despite their youthfulness.

Like me, they are not perfect, and they constantly struggle with the challenges of this technological dispensation coupled with youthful exuberance.

Delano has since got married. God blessed him with a beautiful wife-Denise. My prayer for my children is that they shall remain in fellowship with Jesus Christ and fulfil the purpose for which they were born. I cover them daily with love, prayer and the blood of Jesus.

This is reality, not a cry for sympathy! The call of God sometimes leaves me feeling as if there is no one to care or with whom I can share my troubles. But during those moments, I sense the loving presence of my God, massaging my broken heart and pouring in oil and wine. Hallelujah! He restoreth my soul!

I feel a move in my spirit to encourage someone who is hurting from rejection. More specifically I want to encourage that parent who did all you possibly could for your child or children, and they have rebelled. I am reaching out to the mother who feels abandoned because your child has left home, and you do not even know where he or she is right now.

There is hope for that backslidden daughter living in fornication, adultery, lesbianism or prostitution. There is still hope for your rebellious son who is incarcerated. There is a rope of hope for your children hooked by scamming, drugs, promiscuity, homosexuality or stealing. The juvenile delinquent who has sent a dagger through your heart is coming back home right now in Jesus' name!

The word of God instructs parents in Proverbs 22:6

Train up a child in the way he should go: and when he is old, he will not depart from it.

I want you to come in agreement with me right now that your labour is not in vain in the Lord. Lift your faith in God right now and declare over your children:

> *In the name of Jesus Christ of Nazareth.*
> *(call your child's name) shall live and not die.*
> *(call your child's name) You shall live and declare the works of God.*
> *Father in the name of Your Son Jesus Christ, I ask You to arrest every wayward child right now. Father, please, release high-ranking*

angels to establish a curfew right now Oh God and bring them back from every cardinal point. Make their lives too hot for the enemy to handle Lord.

Please God, release a quick, powerful word in their lives right now Father. Let it pierce and divide their soul and spirit. God send that two-edged sword to the very thoughts and intents of their hearts. Let there be no peace or rest until they surrender to the Lordship of Jesus Christ.

Lord, we thank You for lending them to us. We give them back to You now. Take all the glory, honour and praise for what You have done and will do in and through them now, in Jesus' name.

And all those who believe and claim this victory now say, Amen!

Chapter 7

The Byways and Hedges

Pastor Cynthia Myrie, my spiritual mother describes our early experiences and outdoor evangelistic ministry as we went to the byways and hedges seeking the lost at any cost.

She had this to say:

I met Brother Winston Baker (now Apostle and Bishop) at the Holiness Born Again Apostolic church where I was a member, before his baptism and subsequently becoming a member. I believe I was gifted with the ability to identify greatness, especially in youths. They were drawn to me, and I used the opportunity to mentor them.

That was how Brother Baker, as he was then called, captured my attention. I began studying the word of God with them. They were led into regular prayer and fasting. It was common practice to give them scriptures to study while they fasted. On their return, the scriptures were discussed.

The man of God was easily distinguishable from the other young men, by the number of young children he had with him. He was then married to their mother. His family obligations never hindered him from answering God's call to go to the byways and hedges.

We were always on the go! There was an unforgettable experience on one of our missions in Grange Hill, Westmoreland. Prayer was being offered for an elderly lady when an unclean spirit in the form of a bear manifested. Through the power of the Holy Ghost, the unclean spirit was cast out.

Almost immediately, my cell phone went off. On realizing that the calls were coming from the mother of Apostle Baker's children, I initially ignored them. I thought then that this would be one of her usual calls with the intent to interrupt for no apparent reason. However, I relented and answered the phone when I realized that she was very persistent.

What I heard at the other end of the line sent chills through me. She was screaming at the top of her lungs that an unclean spirit in the form of a gorilla had entered her room. The hideous creature was demanding their second child, Delano. Without hesitation, the room in Grange Hill erupted in warfare prayer and the demon took its flight from their home in Savanna-la-mar.

Now delivered, the elderly lady received the Holy Ghost! Hallelujah! The following day she was taken to the church where she took on the name of Jesus in water baptism. A few weeks afterwards, she exited this stage of life.

Noticeable from those early days was the zeal Bishop Baker had for the Lord. He was rather enthusiastic to increase knowledge of the word, to understand the things about the kingdom of God and yes! To preach the word!

Time has passed and none of those desires has diminished. They have all intensified! Back then, he invited the young men with whom he was acquainted to his house just so he could get an opportunity to minister to them.

God's call on one's life comes with such intensity that it is impossible to ignore and difficult to disobey. I could readily identify with the experience. I too resigned from my job as an insurance sales representative and accepted God's call to full-time ministry. At the time of my resignation, I had just qualified for the coveted 'Million Dollar Round Table' and was scheduled to travel to the USA.

Similarly, as in Apostle Baker's case, I was branded as being crazy for not accepting such a 'great' opportunity. I placed great in quotes because I have come to learn that greatness is relative, depending on whose standards you use to measure it.

From a kingdom perspective, we are aspiring for greatness only when we choose to decrease so that God can increase in our affairs. The result is inexplicable and eternal! Thank God I obeyed! I am excited to see the transformation in the life of my spiritual son since he obeyed likewise.

Having freed myself from my nine-to-five, I became their self-appointed driver, mother and mentor. Meetings were regularly held at Bishop's residence as well as my home in Bath District, Westmoreland. Fasting was done regularly. I still remember the all-night prayer meetings under the big mango tree as if they were yesterday.

Since we were denied entry to the church except for scheduled services, every available location including Bishop Baker's house was utilized as a venue for prayer meetings or preaching points. One thing was guaranteed, the power of the Holy Ghost would be on display. God saved, healed and delivered His people. Everywhere we went and presented the good news, He showed up, confirming His words with mighty signs and wonders.

The favour of God was extended to us by a security guard at Godfrey Stewart High School. As a past employee, I used my connections to gain entrance to a classroom to conduct meetings. The playfield of the adjoining Savanna-la-mar Primary School also became a regular meeting place for prayers.

Travelling was done extensively. We went mostly in groups of five due to the insurance restrictions imposed on my faithful car.

Despite the constant pressure from his family to have him evicted, he worshipped and prayed without ceasing. By now, I realized that his marriage was experiencing turbulence. Not being cognizant of what God was doing in his life, his wife became reluctant to support him in ministry. Constant support had to be provided to maintain a harmonious environment between them.

To say the least, Bishop was consumed with an unrivalled zeal for the byways and hedges. This, however, did not affect his passion for personal evangelism ministry within the local church. With much fervour, he continued tarrying with believers for the infilling of the Holy Ghost. On occasions when the anointing remained on the believer and the church building was being closed, he would place them in the car and continue tarrying with them. Other times they would be taken to his home, where he further ministered to them.

Another popular meeting place was the Fort at the Savanna-la-mar market. While we worshipped there, the crowd would gradually increase around us. There we witnessed several people being saved, delivered and filled with the Holy Ghost. Without the approval of our local church, God used him mightily.

I usually travelled with a bottle of consecrated olive oil. Occasionally, God allowed me to anoint persons at the Savanna-la-mar playfield. There the Lord instructed me to pour the entire bottle on Brother Baker and prophesy over his life. I guess he might recall the things God used me to speak over him.

As his ministry grew, so did religious opposition. The local church body came down quite heavily on me for the support which I provided him. Some members even suggested that they should not be allowed to travel in my car. I stood my ground and guarded him or rather, guarded that which God had placed within him.

Accusations of being of homosexual tendencies were among the darts hurled at him. Even though I was in their midst a lot, the issue was that so many men were always around him. Eventually, people realized that they were being drawn by his passion for the people and things of God.

No sacrifice which I made can compare with what God did in my personal life through this young man's zeal and ministry. My husband was not saved at the time I met Brother Baker. However, as he observed the transformation in this young man's life, he too attested to the fact that God had indeed wrought a miraculous work in his life.

Quite often, Brother Baker would personally minister to my husband. With humility and boldness in the Holy Ghost, he laid his sanctified hands on him and prayed for his salvation. Glory to God! These prayers did not go unanswered. My husband is now a Bishop and the Host Pastor for Anchovy House of Prayer and Praise in the parish of St. James.

Our constant interaction lessened as my husband and I answered God's call to ministry. This led us to a different geographical location. Some time after, I heard of his subsequent fall from grace. I continued to believe that he was destined for greatness in the kingdom of God. As I met and prayed with him, I confirmed that the anointing was still resting heavily on him. Hallelujah!

He returned to the faith, but the enemy came chasing after him; determined to destroy what was left of his character, by any means. But bless God, he was relentless! He oftentimes testified of his legal battle as he faced a possible fifteen (15) year imprisonment term. I was totally convinced that God's hand was still resting on this young man. It was impossible for me to surrender to any coercion to reject him. God had not given up on him and neither would I.

He told me that he was innocent and I believed him! I knew it was the plan of the enemy to destroy him because the accusations came from an incident which occurred almost a year before he surrendered his life to Christ. The devil was grieved with the rapid pace at which he was growing. His potential threat to the kingdom of darkness was evident, the moment he took on the name of Jesus.

At each court date, I presented myself, providing moral and spiritual support. To allow the enemy to sever a bond that God had created was unthinkable, although it was a very trying time. God kept him through it! Glory to God! Today he is a prisoner for Christ who is seeking no bail!

It was an overwhelming, emotional moment to witness the launch of his first book, 'Warring Unclean Spirit'. How much more honoured and humbled I am to be able to share a few of the memories I have from this divine encounter in his fourth publication.

Brother Baker always wanted to be like King David. He was particularly impressed with his life as we studied the lives of various Bible characters. My prayer for him then and now remains, that God will fill him with the spirit of Godly character. I give him the same encouragement that I give myself: Give the glory to God! Never take any for yourself. Every commendation, praise or glory which men ascribe to you, give it to God! Truly God has honoured him and granted the desires of his heart. He is a David indeed!

Today, the ministry of my son in the gospel is well established and my husband and I have been privileged to have him minister at our church. On each visit, the Lord moved mightily and used him in mysterious ways to bring salvation, healing and deliverance to His people. This does not come as a surprise to me because of how desperately he sought God.

He fasted days unendingly! As many as forty-three (43) consecutive days and several seven (7) day absolute fasts – I mean night and day for all the days, he consumed only water. His frail physical frame raised concerns among those who cared about him. While it dwindled from deprivation of natural food, his spirit man was being nourished and grew much larger than those around him.

Numerous testimonies have come back to us from those whose lives were impacted. Among them is recorded proof of someone being healed of Acquired Immune Deficiency Syndrome-AIDS. Hundreds of people witnessed demons being cast out. Dozens of souls surrendered to God and took on the name of Jesus in water baptism.

A gunman who was a hitman/contract killer shared with me how the power of the Holy Ghost landed him on the ground. This was while he still had the gun strapped to his back in a knapsack while Brother Baker was ministering under the unction of the Holy Ghost. He immediately surrendered his life, was baptized in the name of Jesus Christ and later filled with the Holy Ghost. Hallelujah!

Initially, most preachers were sceptical of him. Some accused him of working miracles through witchcraft and necromancy. Over time, God has proven them wrong! This is that which Jesus spoke of in Matthew 10:7-8:

And as ye go, preach, saying, The kingdom of heaven is at hand.

Heal the sick, cleanse the lepers, raise the dead, cast out devils: freely ye have received, freely give.

Needless to say, I am thrilled to note his many accomplishments; but honestly, I am not at all surprised. Brother Baker – now Apostle and Bishop Winston George Baker has journeyed a mighty long way with Jesus. He has endured many afflictions and hard trials, too many to recount. But God kept him! Through many dangers, toils and snares he has already come. Grace brought him to this point and my earnest, fervent prayer, is that God will continue to cover and keep him until that grace brings him safely into eternity.

Chapter 8

The Fall

My failures are too many to mention. I am only alive because of God's grace and mercies. I know that His Agape love is what preserved a wretch like me. There is a rope of hope dangling over you who have fallen so far from grace that you have condemned yourself. Yes, you! I am talking to you right now. God says to tell you, "DON'T DO IT!"

Far be it from me, to recount my failures, misleading anyone into thinking that I am proud of those ungodly actions. Instead, I speak of them, in shame and humility. I am eternally grateful to God for extending mercies to me.

As Paul admonished the Ephesians:

And have no fellowship with the unfruitful works of darkness, but rather reprove them. For it is a shame even to speak of those things which are done of them in secret. Ephesians 5:11-12.

Embedded in my story, is the depth of love that I have experienced from the Lord Jesus Christ. To withhold my testimony of God's faithfulness in marrying the backslider, would therefore be an injustice.

I am all too aware of the condemnatory nature of the church. However, if you are struggling to be reconciled to God, take heart! There is hope! Jesus left all those who were sweetly saved and on their way to glory and came searching in the nightclubs, until He found me. If you have fallen from grace, DO NOT GIVE UP ON YOURSELF! His arms of love are outstretched to you right now. He wants to take you back home.

He gave His life so that you can live. Once you are reading this book, you are not too far gone. God says, "GET UP! BRUSH YOURSELF OFF! GET BACK IN THE RACE!" Who says that you cannot make it? That is a lie from the pit of hell! Of course, you can make it! I decree and declare that you will make it in the name of Jesus!

I fell into the trap of adultery. Overcome with embarrassment, I could not face the many persons I had disappointed. I was also not prepared to face those who would be rejoicing and waiting for every opportunity to remind me of my fall from grace. I subsequently left the church. Sure, you are familiar with both sets, if you have been in church long enough. But who knows that it is not over until God says it's over?

Chapter 9
The Re-Call

I vividly recall a visitation from God when He told me: "Before I formed thee in the belly I knew thee, and before thou camest forth out of the womb I sanctified thee, and I ordained thee a prophet unto the nations." I told you before that I am pre-destined. Therefore, whatever the devil meant for evil, God would sooner or later turn it into good so that He can get His glory.

Satan is an accuser, he uses tactics to plant seeds of doubt, fear, depression and oppression in the lives of God's people. However, when you are predestined as I am, God will make a way. We may not know how He plans to do it, but He will.

So, I left the church and before long returned to my previous passion. Dancing and partying once again became my routine. Only God knew how much I hated being in that backslidden state. Nonetheless, I continued as though I was doing great. For so I thought, until one night, the Lord visited me.

The members of the dance group had gathered at my home for one of the usual nights of rehearsal, talk and laughter. We were there enjoying ourselves until I felt my spirit connected with that of my Lord and Saviour. He said, "Son, when do you plan to come back to me?" I responded, "Lord, as soon as mi mek some money and become rich den mi wi consider coming back." He said, "OK, you got that right, you will make money from dancing and become rich, but you will die rich at age forty-three."

What he did next was frightening. He showed me scene by scene how I would meet my demise. There was a feeling of wonder and amazement. It was difficult for me to understand how the Holy Ghost, who I thought would have been taken away from me the moment I backslid, was still so evidently with me. However, in this undone condition, I discovered that having taken on the name of Jesus, I was permanently marked. I was ignorant of the fact that I still did not belong to myself. Jesus had redeemed me years ago with His rich, efficacious blood and despite my failures, I remained His son.

I could not fathom being dead at forty-three. I will admit that I had great plans to make some well-needed money. The wealth I amassed would transform the unsuitable living conditions of my four 'handbags' whom I was single-handedly raising. 'Handbags' was the term by which some church folks referenced my children. They were too young for me to leave, especially in the manner which God revealed to me.

I could not die at forty-three! No way! Not with the words that were spoken over my life before I fell from grace. I was now determined that by the grace of God, and with every fibre of my being, I would withstand the wiles of the enemy. I reminded myself of Jeremiah 1: 5 – I shall prophesy to the nations. I told myself God shall use me to win souls for His kingdom and I must fulfil my God-given purpose on earth.

After that moment, I quickly came back to the earth realm. Without hesitation, I told the members of the dance group that I am done with dancing. I am done with this current lifestyle. No more rehearsals and no more partying. I'm done! I am going back to church.

They thought I was going crazy. They were shocked to hear this, especially since our earlier discussion was about dance routines for upcoming events. Despite all of that, I was serious about my decision. I couldn't afford to die at forty-three! I chose instead to live and declare the works of the Lord.

I subsequently relayed to them, the encounter I had with Jesus while they were having a good time. They were now bewildered at the wonders of God. They encouraged me to return to God and promised to join me at church in the future.

So, like the lost sheep that was later found, I returned to the sheepfold. Have I been perfect since then? No! Not at all! At all! At all! But by His grace, I am determined to make it. Daily I ask Him to purify me and draw me even closer to His precious bleeding side. I live on repentance ground and endeavour to avoid situations and persons whom I discern are tools assigned by the enemy to destroy my life. Thank God for Overseer Mullings! (formerly Alcapone of our Dance group) who remains committed to our friendship, serving the Lord and working alongside me in ministry. Because of his faithfulness to God, he has been blessed with his own home, car, a beautiful wife and children.

I continue to pray and crave the prayers of well-meaning believers. We must bear each other's burden to make it. God bless all who prayed for me in my fallen state. I love you!

Right now, as I think of the goodness of Jesus and all He has done for me, I would be ungrateful not to pause for a Praise Break!

PRAISE BREAK

He brought me out, Hallelujah!
He brought me out, Glory to God!
He brought me out, Oh praise His Holy name!
Help me celebrate Jesus Christ
The Omnipotent One
The Omniscient One
The Omnipresent One
The only potentate
My God who brought me out!
Clap your hands and open your mouth
Magnify the Lord with me
Worship the Lord of lords
Worship the conquering Lion of the Tribe of Judah
Glorify the Most High God

He is worthy to be praised, Hallelujah!
Give God the highest praise
Praise the Most-High God
Praise the God of Abraham
Lift up the God of Isaac
Praise Israel's God
Praise the God of Elijah
Praise Daniel's God
Praise Winston George Baker's God
From rejection, He brought me out
From jail, He brought me out
From the pit, He brought me out
From the fall, He brought me out
From obscurity, He brought me out
From the guttermost, He brought me out
Help me praise Him
Hallelujah
You are at the right place at the right time for your miracle!
You are at the right place at the right time for your breakthrough!
Glory to God!

PART 2

THE UTTERMOST

Chapter 10

The Backside of the Desert

In May 2009, God led me to Hide Away Lane to tend to a flock of eight (8) sheep. Three of whom had strayed from the fold, leaving five faithful ones. Indeed, He is a God of wisdom! That is all I imagined I could care for at that time. I was accustomed to caring for a family of five, (my four children and myself). Perfect start! I concluded, despite my fears.

Given the significance of numbers, in the realm of the spirit, I realized God had strategically placed me in this location. Also, the name of the community was of great significance. It was a perfect description of the environment. God was 'hiding me away' so that I could practice what He deposited in me to manage my biological family of five and my church family of five children.

There were more similarities than I cared to note between the two families. The mother of this family was also overseas. But! through the grace of God, I made it, and I must say that I am eternally grateful for the opportunity that was given to me to be the under-shepherd of this flock.

Without any doubt in my mind, God had opened the heart of His daughter at that point to receive me as a son in Christ. Her placing me over the flock in her absence was divinely orchestrated to develop leadership qualities, Godliness and integrity in me. My love and gratitude towards this woman of God continue to flow unceasingly. She believed in me when most others did not. God allowed her to give me an opportunity to grow when others would not.

My fervent prayer is that God will bless her abundantly. What I am in Christ today can be partly attributed to the grace of God on my life in 'Hide Away Lane'. This woman of God's obedience to the voice of God opened a door that no man can shut! Hallelujah!

My steps are ordered by the Lord. No doubt about that! Five is a very significant number in biblical numerology. Man was created with five fingers, five toes and five senses. The number five is the number of God's grace. I pointed out to you that my biological family consisted of five persons at the time I went to Hide Away Lane and I was placed to care for five sheep.

Only the grace of God could have been accredited for the many things that He wrought through me in that little ministry for the three and a half years which I spent there. All my experiences informed my approach to church leadership today. That was good! But the power of God on my life in the backside of the desert blew my cover!

Before long, 'Hide Away Lane' was found! People filed in by the dozens to receive their breakthrough. God's presence and power were so potent in that place. It was explosive! Untold miracles took place. Some of these happened many times without even touching the afflicted. The atmosphere was supercharged from the worship that went straight up to the third heavens.

Stirred by our worship, God stepped from His throne and manifested in our midst through the dissecting of His word. I was and remain His mouthpiece. What He released through my lips was according to Hebrews 4:12:-

For the word of God is quick, and powerful, and sharper than any two edged sword, piercing even to the dividing asunder of soul and spirit, and of the joints and marrow, and is a discerner of the thoughts and intents of the heart.

The potency of the Word led sinners to repentance, opened blinded eyes, brought deliverance to those who were bound by witchcraft, healed the sick, opened doors the enemy had shut, broke curses and poured blessings on God's people.

Distance became no barrier to people who were desperate to see and experience the move of God.

I recall an instance where a man took his wife from the hospital in Black River after she had received seven strokes. Her left side was completely dead. He was warned that within minutes of removing her from professional care, she would experience another stroke.

This desperate husband was still determined to exercise his faith in God. The authorities requested that he document his intentions. This was to ensure that the hospital would not be held liable for what the doctors perceived to be inevitable-her deterioration or death. He complied and left the hospital with his wife.

On reaching the church, four brothers assisted in removing her from the vehicle by placing her on a chair which they lifted and placed in the church. Her husband stood next to her left side to keep her body in an upright position on the chair.

The church continued to worship and the anointing fell on an eight-year-old girl. She led a march around the building giving high praises and worship to God. I was instructed by the Holy Ghost to place my wet rag -filled with my perspiration- on her head.

What happened thereafter, remains a mystery to medical practitioners and doubters until today. Firstly, she threw her left hand in the air. In amazement, I asked, rhetorically "God, which hand is that?" Before I could ascertain which hand it was, she jumped to her feet and began running around the church, magnifying the name of Jesus.

Those kinds of miracles are indeed astounding, but nothing compares with the miracle of salvation! Being overwhelmed is a rather simple way to describe the feeling

I experience when the transformational power of the blood of Jesus is being displayed. Glory be to God! So they believed, so they were baptized! And the Lord added to the church daily such as should be saved.

Miraculously, that little structure housed over two hundred persons on service nights. Drawn by the astounding power of God, they came from all walks of life. Just as He did with me, He pulled hundreds from the pit to the pulpit. I must hasten to say that I am not trying to compare the quality and achievements of my ministry in 'Hide Away Lane' with Jesus' ministry. However, like Jesus, I did three and a half years there before I was crucified.

After my resurrection, I was instructed to relocate from what the enemy would have wanted to make a permanent tomb. God instructed me to go to the highway. He taught me to be more focused on what He was doing than the opposition. By this time, I was even more eager to see a greater manifestation of the power of God.

The nearly five hundred souls that were baptized in water, taking on the name of Jesus, only served to whet my appetite, not to mention the numerous persons being filled with the Holy Ghost and fire. I was now ready to demonstrate the power of my Holy Ghost given Ph.D - Preach, Heal, Deliver- to the ends of the earth!

You know I was not formally trained at any religious institution. It follows, therefore, that I have no man-made documentation of any theological accreditation.

Remember that I did not graduate from any formal educational institution. By men's standards, I have no academic achievement. I am not qualified, at all! at all! at all!

Boldly I can stand and declare, however, without fear of being refuted, that I have my Ph.D. This is that which I received according to the faithfulness of God in fulfilling the promise made in Joel 2:28.

And it shall come to pass afterward, that I will pour out My Spirit upon all flesh; and your sons and your daughters shall prophesy, your old men shall dream dreams, your young men shall see visions.

I am so glad that God did not use my physical frame to determine the measure of His Spirit that He would pour out on me. Neither do my human frailties limit the demonstration of His power at work through me. He saw it fitting to bestow on me after three and a half years of intensive training in the backside of the desert, a Ph.D. for the highway.

As I left Hide Away Lane, He said to me: I have called you as a prophet to the nations. Go!

P-REACH

H-EAL and

D-ELIVER

Self-praise is no recommendation! God, however, continues to confirm the words He speaks through me with mighty signs and wonders. Glory to God!

Chapter 11

From the Pit to the Pulpit

Today, whenever I preach, I inform the congregation that I am not a sermonette preacher. In the pulpit, I am simply a messenger of the Lord Jesus Christ. The job of the FEDEX brother is like mine. I simply deliver the message God gives me to deliver and keep moving.

Whomever God calls to be a prophet or an apostle usually gets divine visitations. The end of the year is usually one such time for this supernatural encounter. This is because God is a God of time even though He is eternal. The devil cannot stop our God! Whenever God decrees a thing, no devil in hell can nullify it!

As in the beginning, God continues to reveal His plans for His people to His servants today. The Bible would have us know in Amos 3:7

The Lord GOD will do nothing, but He revealeth His secret unto His servants the prophets.

God would, therefore, deposit His secrets in the hearts of His prophets. The prophets would then release the word to the people. God would then perform it. God does things timely!

Towards the end of the year 2012, the Lord told me to move from the church I had been pastoring. Admittedly, I was rather fearful of my ability to establish what God was downloading into my spirit. Given the history of the church, I began to prayerfully seek God's direction to commence the process.

The instruction from God was to "Leave well." I was directed to construct a letter which should include my gratitude for the opportunity to serve in that ministry. Additionally, I was to express my decision to obey God's direction to relocate to a new area of the vineyard. Finally, I should indicate the time of my departure, allowing enough time for a replacement to be found for me.

I did as I was commanded and at the appointed time I left. Immediately after leaving, all hell broke loose. Having endured many harsh and unpleasant circumstances before, I somewhat fooled myself into believing that it could not have got worse. Boy, I was dead wrong!

The reality of 'hell on earth' began at this point in my life and ministry. So many evil things were said about me. The very persons who once hailed me a great man of God began to say that I am an obeah man. All the miracles for which God got the glory previously, were now said to have been accomplished through witchcraft.

Friends became major enemies, and every effort was made to hinder the work that God had sent me to do. It was reported to the police that I was establishing the church illegally and that it should be shut down immediately. What the enemy did not know was that God had placed two lawyers in the ministry's head office in Kingston for such a time as this.

They had favoured King Jesus Pentecostal Fellowship by registering the ministry to establish fifty churches in Jamaica. You see, God told me that this would be the first mega-church in western Jamaica. Now, God said it! I believe it! So, guess what? That settles it! Like Nehemiah, I continued to build the walls of the church, while Sanballat and Tobiah continued to plot and scheme.

A young man who had just returned from prison visited the church and got baptized. He requested to speak with me at the end of the service. In the privacy of my office, the young man informed me that he was in jail at the Negril Police Station when a bishop and a pastor came demanding that the church be shut down immediately. At this point, we were worshipping in a little container with blue tarpaulin. The ministry had no money at all!

A well-known obeah man was among those who decided that this ministry must not survive. His anger was kindled because his once thriving business was now far less appealing. Many persons who once wasted thousands of dollars to get help from the dark world were now surrendering their lives to Jesus. Their deliverance was received through the power in the name of Jesus, free of cost.

Later, I was informed that there were numerous attempts to bring my life to an end through the assignment of demonic forces. All failed! Praise God! In desperation, a hitman was paid to blow my brain out. But that too failed! Glory be to God! I am still here because God kept me! I had the privilege to pray for this particular hitman. He demanded that I prayed for him in the presence of seven young men who were with him.

God told me years ago that He was going to give me something that all my haters would see and covet. However, He assured me that they would not be able to do anything about it if I remained in Him. There is work for me to do and I am determined to finish it. I am unstoppable!

Amid all the persecution, the church grew rapidly. There was a man of God who usually introduced me as a son in the gospel. In introducing me to a congregation, he described me as the man of God who possessed the eyes of an eagle and could see through six-inch walls. Surprisingly, out of nowhere, he too turned against me.

Had it not been for the Lord's constant reminder, not to put my trust in man, I would have fainted in disbelief. This same man of God accused me of practising witchcraft. If that were not enough, he began a dreadful rumour that I had received a potion from a witch to place in the baptismal pool. This is what he claimed was responsible for the numerous persons taking on the name of Jesus in water baptism. Additionally, he stood in the midst of a congregation and declared from the pulpit that God told him that I was a homosexual. He went on further to say that God told Him that He is going to kill me.

I was shocked to hear the utterance, but as painful as it was, I decided to take it for Jesus.

At our next service, a missionary got up and prophesied for the first time. Under the anointing of the Holy Ghost, she declared, "God says that He is the One who called you and He is going to kill somebody to shut the mouth of all who have risen up against you."

Within three days of this prophetic utterance, the minister who prophesied that God was going to kill me lost his wife. She fell ill suddenly and did not recover. The sad news spread rapidly throughout the churches. People began to associate his calamity with his evil utterances against me. Immediately, the evil reports aimed at destroying my reputation as a servant of God subsided.

I don't even feel compelled to defend myself against that particular accusation. However, I will make the following declaration just in case you are questioning my sexual orientation. I speak the truth in Christ and I lie not; the Holy Ghost bearing me witness. From the day that I was placed on this earth, I have never and by God's grace, will never be sexually attracted to a male.

Accusations most times make me smile. As they arise, the Lord of heaven who called and sanctified me, gives me peace, deep within my soul. Whenever I preach that there are some wicked church people, it is no joke; neither is it an unfounded statement. I have felt the cruel hands of death and destruction from people who preach, prophesy and speak in more tongues than the Apostle Paul.

Despite the persecution, I continue to preach and God continues to confirm His words with signs and wonders. Like Phillip, I will continue preaching the powerful message of the kingdom of God amid the pressure. Phillip remained available to be used by God, even after his house was burnt down. God used him in a mighty way to bring the Ethiopian eunuch into a relationship with Jesus Christ.

Holy Ghost 'dunamis' power has taken me over and I just cannot keep silent. People are amazed at how I preach God's word so boldly despite possessing such a reserved personality. The truth is that I am mantled! Under the unction of the Holy Ghost, I am merely a conduit. This little lump of clay is just the hose and the gloves that God uses to manifest His awesome power in the earth realm.

It is a rare privilege, and it keeps me humbled. I am not my own, I belong to Jesus! A long time ago I told Jesus that I will be His jackass. Daily I ask Him to saddle me with the power of the Holy Ghost and sit on me. Without murmuring or complaining, I promise to go wherever He leads. The greatest satisfaction I have ever experienced in this life is God performing wonders through me. Nothing in this world compares to the awesome moments in the supernatural realm. Neither would I exchange it for family, financial status or academic achievement. You can have the world but give me Jesus!

There are occasions when I can see people in the realm of the Spirit, who come to the services to 'check me out'. Most times, as the dunamis stretch out in me and begins to manifest, they become believers themselves. Awesome! Isn't it?

These are some of the testimonies which excite me most. For that reason, I try to avoid meeting with persons who attend the services, before I preach. I'm not just excited to preach. I am even more excited about Jesus being glorified and watching the jaws of unbelievers drop in disbelief when the spectacular power of God is on display and naysayers are silenced.

God is truly amazing! I met Him in the pit years ago and I now have the distinct and indescribable pleasure of watching Him use me in the pulpit. I have witnessed so many miracles, I will not be able to mention but a few during this publication. Guess what? Deep down in my sanctified soul, I believe that greater things are still to come. God has revealed to me that He is going to use me to raise the dead after postmortem! I cannot wait!

Chapter 12

Reigning as King and Priest

I have experienced some switches in my life, resulting in improvements in my standard of living. Despite all of this, by choice, I remain humble because I know the irony of material gain. The same hand that gives is the same hand that takes away. Hence, in whatever state I am, I learn to be contented. Like Paul, I know how to abase and how to abound. I know what it is to be full, but I lived most of my past life in dire need.

God has graciously made those few switches to bring glory and honour to His name. I am just the beneficiary of His grace and mercy. He has entrusted me with a few things to serve His people. Therefore, I pray earnestly that He grants me the wisdom, knowledge and understanding which equip me to be a good steward. I pray for strength and resilience to finish every assignment well. Those who understand the magnitude of such responsibility understand the importance of being constantly prayerful.

I was confined to a colourless BMX bicycle most of my life. I loved it and still do. Every now and then I still take a ride through the town. In school, 'X' is used to indicate that an answer is wrong. I had too many things wrong in my life, so God gave me a switch! He replaced the 'X' with a 'W'. That was just God's little way of showing me that I was a winner from the womb. Contrary to what the devil wanted me to believe, I am not a mistake. My entry into the world was by divine design.

God switching the BMX to a BMW was a coveted change. Nonetheless, I will not be distracted by God's grace. You see, the value of material things fades into oblivion when it is compared to the glory of Jesus! Hallelujah!

As God remained faithful, I was later blessed with two Mercedes Benz within two years. One night after delivering a message titled "Raising up an Altar", I went home and was checking my WhatsApp messages. To my surprise, I came upon two separate mind-blowing messages. One listener testified of being led to bless me with a Porsche and the other of being led to bless me with a 15-seater bus. Praise be to God! Both vehicles are now in my possession.

God has significantly improved my living condition. Glory to God! Until recently, I was still occupying the same family house at 11 Segree Street in Savanna-la-mar. This is where I have been living for most of my years since I was eight.

My goodness, I wouldn't have enough space and time in this book to detail all the controversy, contention and embarrassment that I have dealt with during this period. As recently as a year before penning this book, one of my sisters had me in court again. This was her third or fourth attempt to get the court to evict me from the place I have called home most of my life. Along with the use of witchcraft, she has been relentless in her pursuits to have me vacate the premises; but God blocked it every time.

In late 2022, I was faced with another dilemma which compounded the already uncomfortable situation. A family member who was caring for my incapacitated brother placed him back at this house in my care. This was rather overwhelming, but God granted me grace until a more suitable arrangement was put in place for his care.

The devil tried all kinds of tricks, but I saw them as mere distractions. It remains true that the gates of hell cannot prevail against the church. Praise God! I have lived to testify that God has blessed me to purchase the adjoining property -13 Segree Street, Savanna-la-mar. I am now the legitimate owner of a six-bedroom home that onlookers have dubbed, "A Castle for the Apostle".

Look at that! God took me from the three-bedroom family house where I wasn't welcomed, to a six-bedroom house. Double for my trouble indeed! Just-like-that! This is just the beginning because God promised me seven houses! Yes, you heard me right! I believe it and am patiently waiting on His perfect timing for the fulfilment of this promise.

Understandably, some are concerned about my choice to remain in the ghetto. I truly appreciate your thoughtfulness. But guess what? This is where God has planted me and His instruction to me is, "Son – Bloom where you are planted."

The ways in which God blessed me during the construction of that house still have me in awe. I witnessed the house going up without any knowledge of how some of the building materials were acquired. On numerous occasions, the builder would say, "Sir, I got this today." To my amazement, there was sand, blocks, gravel and cement which I did not purchase. Glory to the name of the ever-faithful God!

At one point the builder requested building materials costing approximately one million dollars. Without any idea of where the funds were coming from, I said to him, "OKAY!" I had no knowledge, but God knew because He is my source. It didn't stop there. I learnt the items were needed by the next business day.

Sure enough, God miraculously intervened. On my way from church in Kingston that Sunday, I got a call from a member of the church. I was asked to stop by the person's home to collect some money. Believe it or not, I received just the amount of money that was needed to complete the transaction.

I know that the devil will still try, but I too will not relent. God rewards faithfulness. I implore you to remain faithful to God, if you suffer with Him, you shall reign with him.

In the King Jesus Pentecostal Fellowship, I have witnessed God shifting in several ways. The Kingston

Branch-Headquarters- was relocated from Patrick Gardens to Red Hills Road. The seating capacity of the previous building was just two hundred. Now God has blessed us with a house able to accommodate fifteen hundred persons.

Not only that, but His divine providence also continues to be evident with the payment of the rental for this new building. This has increased from under Fifty Thousand dollars a month at the previous location to almost Five Hundred Thousand per month. With man, it seems impossible, but our God provides wherever He guides. Glory be to God!

I am not boasting but I report victory in the lives of my children too! They have all successfully completed secondary education and two began to pursue tertiary studies. The youngest is completing her final year at the University of the West Indies and by God's grace, she will be graduating with honours. Except for one, they are in full-time ministry. My children's eagerness to pursue the knowledge of God is admirable! Given my experience with God, I am excited and supportive of their decision to put God first.

My life is a living testimony of His faithfulness in adding all things to those who obey His instructions. We have by no means arrived! But things are already way better than they used to be. The season of hunger and nakedness is over! Praise God!

David said in Psalm 1:1-3:

> *Blessed is the man that walketh not in the counsel of the ungodly, nor standeth in the way of sinners, nor sitteth in the seat of the scornful.*
>
> *But his delight is in the law of the Lord; and in His law doth he meditate day and night.*
>
> *And he shall be like a tree planted by the rivers of water, that bringeth forth his fruit in his season; his leaf also shall not wither; and whatsoever he doeth shall prosper.*

I shall not be moved! I shall not be moved! I shall not be moved! Hallelujah! By the grace of God, I shall remain in the place where God has planted me. By God's grace, I shall be fruitful there. And by God's grace, I shall be used to colonize every person in this ghetto who will be obedient to the Spirit of Almighty God resting on my life.

There is nothing wrong with people leaving the ghetto for a better life whenever God opens a door for them. However, I am opposed to those who have gone out and forgot those who have been left behind struggling. God has ignited a fire within me to change the ghetto. However, it is not a change from without but rather a change from within.

This is a clarion call to all the ghetto youths like me. We are no longer looking at what man can do for us. We believe that there is an Almighty God who has moulded us in His image and wrapped up purpose inside us. There is within each of us the power to prosper and get wealth once we reconnect to our source.

I realize that many of you have already come full circle, putting down the guns and walking with Jesus. We have been enslaved for far too long, believing that the change we so desperately desire is supposed to come from someone who pities our condition.

Just a few years ago, I used to be locked away in all-night prayer with approximately one hundred men on Tuesday nights at Loving Care Christian Academy in Savanna la Mar. This we did religiously after enjoying an awesome game of football and a sumptuous meal. That gave me great joy! It was awesome to see souls, especially of men reaching out for Christ as deer pants for water. It is time to go back to our Creator and give our lives to Him. Let Him repair the damaged way of thinking and believing and show us who we are and what we were meant to be.

Revelation 1:5-6 says:

> *And from Jesus Christ, who is the faithful witness, and the first begotten of the dead, and the Prince of the kings of the earth. Unto Him that loved us, and washed us from our sins in His own blood,*
> *And hath made us kings and priests unto God and His Father, to Him be glory and dominion forever and ever, Amen.*

This powerful word now informs who I am. I, WINSTON GEORGE BAKER have been made a KING AND PRIEST! I am in the ghetto but the ghetto mentality no longer enslaves me. I am free in Jesus' name! That which was once used to shackle me now lays at my feet. I am now seated in the uttermost! Hallelujah! This is a great moment for a praise break if you can relate.

Ephesians 2:4-10:

> *But God, who is rich in mercy, for His great love wherewith He loved us,*
>
> *Even when we were dead in sins, hath quickened us together with Christ (by grace ye are saved)*
>
> *And hath raised us up together, and made us sit together in heavenly places in Christ Jesus:*
>
> *That in the ages to come He might shew the exceeding riches of His grace in His kindness toward us through Christ Jesus,*
>
> *For by grace are ye saved through faith; and that not of yourselves: it is the gift of God:*
>
> *Not of works, lest any man should boast.*
>
> *For we are His workmanship, created in Christ Jesus unto good works, which God hath before ordained we should walk in them.*

This is the information which transformed my life and my circumstances. It comes directly from the Manufacturer's manual. You must understand where you came from. Who made you? God made me and wisdom dictates that I search the Holy Scriptures for the answers to my life's questions. Along with the production of goods, is the preparation of a manual which provides important information. For the optimal benefit to be derived from the product, the purchaser is advised to read and adhere to the instructions in the manual.

If the product refuses to function as it was designed to, the purchaser is instructed to return it to the manufacturer. This cannot be truer about man and God. Hopeless and helpless are those persons who look to every other source for help, but God. Until man acknowledges their Creator and through His word, gets direction for life, every contrary path taken will lead to failure.

Some persons appear to be thriving without God. Some have amassed wealth by illegal means; glory in it to the shame of others who remain impoverished. Do not be fooled! This will not last! Check them out too, because if they choose to be truthful, they will admit that they are miserable!

Not everyone who emerged from the ghetto with wealth is involved in illegal activities. However, wealth without God leaves a person spiritually impoverished.
Revelation 3:17-18

> *Because thou sayest, I am rich and increased with goods, and need nothing; and knowest not that thou art wretched, and miserable, and poor, and blind, and naked:*
>
> *I counsel thee to buy of Me gold tried in the fire, that thou mayest be rich; and white raiment, that thou mayest be clothed, and that the shame of thy nakedness do not appear; and anoint thine eyes with eyesalve, that thou mayest see.*
>
> *As many as I love, I rebuke and chasten; be zealous therefore, and repent.*

I know that some people are disappointed by my abstinence from offering get-rich-quick tips or any money management advice. This is not an oversight! It is deliberate because the truth is, I can only give that which I have received.

Recently, I have been observing, with much sorrow, the manner of speech of some well-known international preachers. They began in storefronts and basements with less than ten members, including their wives and children. What God placed on them was the anointing to preach, heal and deliver. However, this same anointing eventually brings material blessings into their lives.

Sadly, they begin to purport the blessings of God as wealth obtained by their wisdom and human efforts. These once tongue-talking; holy rollers have become so sophisticated that one would need to keep a dictionary at hand, to understand the message. Others have become merely motivational speakers. All this is happening while the world is groaning to see the manifestation of the sons of God.

Jesus promised in John 14:12-14:

> *Verily, verily, I say unto you, He that believeth on Me, the works that I do shall he do also; and greater works than these shall he do; because I go unto My Father.*
>
> *And whatsoever ye shall ask in My name, that will I do, that the Father may be glorified in the Son.*
>
> *If ye shall ask any thing in My name, I will do it.*

This is what the world is waiting to see! Forgive me if this sounds like an attack on the clergy. It is not! But I cannot apologize if it provokes preachers to get back to the basics, where it is all about Jesus and not about us.

Far be it from me to boast of anything that God has entrusted to my care. I am cognizant of the fact that I am just a steward. Everything is to be used as a testimony that 'HE IS FAITHFUL AND HE IS ABLE!' I am here to declare my assets and my position in Christ Jesus. My greatest assets are the Holy Ghost and dunamis power. My present position is being seated in the uttermost with Christ Jesus after being elevated from the guttermost!

Do not view me as being greater or better than you because of my transformation. God is just using me to direct or redirect you to your source so that we can be in this together. There is no need for you to be covetous or jealous and there is no need for me to be selfish. The good news is, our God can never go broke! The cattle on a thousand hills belong to Him.

That explains why I do not compare myself with others, whether saved or unsaved. Neither do I compete with others. The kingdom of God does not promote selfishness. God intends for us to have all things in common. One of the things that God uses to test whether He can trust a believer, is giving him wealth. The passing or failing of that test is evident in how we treat others, especially those who are in need.

My mandate as a king and priest is to colonize people who are living with a ghetto mentality. Everywhere God sends me to represent Him, I preach this good news of the Kingdom of God. Unlike worldly men, I want every ghetto youth to come and experience what I am experiencing. That is the purpose of this book.

Many people testify about my life, without knowing the truth. Some do it with evil intentions; others for good. Now, you are hearing it from me! This is my story! Despite our different situations, it can become yours too. If you are sick and tired of your situation, get up and do what I did.

Right where you are at this moment, STOP! Get on your knees and surrender all to Jesus! Let Him direct it from here. I guarantee you that your life will never be the same. I do not care who you are. If Jesus is not the Lord of your life, you are lost! Some of you are focused on money but God wants you to be focused on Him and being a citizen of His kingdom. He has an impeccable record of providing for His citizens.

Let me pray with and for you as you surrender all to Jesus:

> **Father in the name of Jesus Christ of Nazareth, thank you for Your creation who now returns to his source. Now Oh Lord God of heaven, wash away his sins with Your rich, red, efficacious blood.**
>
> **Father, I present him to You for redemption, reconciliation and restoration. Order his steps to bring glory and honour to Your name.**
>
> **We thank You that all his needs are met in You, according to Your faithfulness to Your word spoken in Matthew 6:33**
>
> **But seek ye first the kingdom of God, and His righteousness; and all these things shall be added unto you.**
>
> **Lord God of heaven and earth be pleased to take all the glory, honour and**

**praise as Your son/Your daughter returns
to the fold, in Jesus' mighty name.
Amen**

Hallelujah! Heaven is throwing a party right now just for you! That is what God does each time one of His creations comes back to its Source for redirection.

Welcome my brother! Welcome my sister! We are all now one in the kingdom of God. As His dear son, He now wants to give you the key to live a successful life for time and eternity. God bless you.

Just before we go to the next level, allow God to lead you to a Bible-believing church. One that is led by the Holy Ghost and which is on fire for God. If you are not yet baptized in the name of Jesus, you need to do so now.

Now let us go discover the key to a prosperous life!

Chapter 13

The Key

Jesus knew full well who He was and yet He avoided self-glorification at all costs. As my example, I follow suit. This admonishment was also given by Apostle Paul to the believers in Philippi and remains sound advice for all true worshippers.

> *Let this mind be in you, which was also in Christ Jesus:*
> *Who, being in the form of God, thought it not robbery to be equal with God:*
> *But made Himself of no reputation, and took upon Him the form of a servant, and was made in the likeness of men:*
> *And being found in fashion as a man, He humbled Himself, and became obedient unto death, even the death of the cross.*
> Philippians 2:5-8

Being a follower of Christ, I am simply amazed at the power of the word of God. Yielding to the power of the Word of God has brought tremendous benefits to my life. Everything that God uses me to do, reveals the genius of

God in a body given over to Him. When He is through with me on any given assignment, I go home and reflect on all the wonders God performed. It is such a humbling experience.

For this reason, I beg all those whose lives God has touched through me, to give all the glory to Jesus. Truly, I cannot take any for myself and more importantly, God is a jealous God! I have watched with regret, many persons who were once used by God in powerful ways, fall from grace. I cry to God in desperation, to keep my feet on a straight path. I pray earnestly that my eyes will be kept on Him and that I will remain humble.

As painful as the persecutions are, I thank God for them. They keep me on my knees. They serve as constant reminders of how badly the devil wants to destroy me. The message in this book cannot be about me. It must be about what God has done and continues to do in me. Its primary purpose is to increase the God who made all things possible and to reduce me. In sharing my transformation details, I must first introduce you to the Transformer. He is Jesus Christ of Nazareth, Son of the Living God.

Please excuse my unapologetic excitement and exuberance when I begin to talk about Jesus. Forgive me if you did not get the Holy Ghost and fire baptism which I received. I have been set ablaze and this fire just won't go out. It has taken me over and literally consumes my entire being. I am C-R-A-Z-Y about Jesus!

Many times, the power of the Holy Ghost uses my story to tranquillize others and end up transforming them too. Hallelujah! That's my earnest prayer for you also.

Recently, I was in a Sunday night service at one of our local churches. A gentleman, who experienced God's miraculous power in the ministry, took several young men from a neighbouring parish to the church. He lined them out in the front row and they sat there attentively.

The Lord had me teach briefly from one of the books I authored-The Kingdom Mandate Handbook. Its purpose is to remind readers of who they are and whose they are. However, its main emphasis is on guiding them into establishing their God-given purpose and fulfilling it.

When I was through, I invited those who needed to accept Jesus as their Lord and Saviour to an altar of prayer. The young men all came forward. Somehow, the Holy Ghost directed me to share a particular aspect of my life, before instructing me to go to the baptismal pool. I obeyed both commands and God showed up and delivered every one of them.

Before that night was over, ten persons were baptized in Jesus' name and went back to their world to colonize it. Glory to God! My God from Zion! This is only the smoke of what I am believing God to continue to accomplish through the power of the Holy Ghost as this book is being read.

The dead shall be raised! Blind eyes shall pop open! Deaf ears shall be unstopped! All manner of sicknesses and diseases shall be healed! Souls shall be saved! Lives shall be transformed! Many shall be filled with the Holy Ghost and fire! You shall be renewed! Yes, you shall be refreshed! Glory to God! You shall be revived in Jesus' name!

The power of the Holy Ghost in this book is going to ignite fresh fire! "A revival shall break out!" says the Lord. Glory to God! He is doing a new thing! He is fast-forwarding His mandate! The Kingdom of God is stepping over the religious folks and going after those who are hungry to see the move of God.

It is overtaking the prostitutes, scammers, gunmen and those who are despised. God is raising them up as an army in these last days to bring glory and honour to His name. Signs and wonders shall follow them. Not because they are influential. Not because they are educated. Not because they are from a good family background. Not at all! At all! At all!

God shall raise them up because they believe on Jesus and are willing to reject religion in pursuit of a relationship with God. These are hungry folks! These are angry folks! Angry because of what the enemy has stolen from them. Hungry because they are desperate for a change. Folks who are hungry and angry are prime candidates for dunamis power. Once filled with dunamis, they are UNSTOPPABLE! That's me right there! Are you one of them?

I am a monotheist. This word is derived from two Greek words: 'monos' which means one, single or alone and 'theos' which means God. There is only one God. His name is Jesus! This is what I believe and I serve the One God. I paused to make that profound declaration because it is imperative that you understand how important numbers are to God.

God could have spoken everything into existence on the very first day of creation. Instead, He did it in His own time, using six days. Numbers have biblical significance as explained in biblical numerology. Here are some examples:

One refers to God being absolute. This is the origin of the Hebrew teachings on monotheism
Two refers to division; order
Three refers to manifestations
Four refers to discipline
Five refers to grace, mercy and truth
Six refers to man
Seven refers to perfection; completion
Eight refers to new beginnings
Nine refers to gifts
Ten refers to judgment

In Egypt, God used ten plagues to release His judgment upon this nation. The tithes, which is a tenth of one's earnings, is referred to as the accursed portion. Noah's generation was the tenth from Adam and the flood they experienced was the judgment of God.

Towards the end of the year 2015, I was reflecting on some prophecies which were fulfilled in that year. I had prophesied that some persons in our congregation would be blessed with cars. I vividly remember receiving testimonies of seven cars miraculously landing in the lives of God's people.

The Lord told me to prophesy that houses would be received. Glory be to God! Five houses were miraculously placed in the hands of God's children. Under the leading of the Holy Ghost, I released a word over the believers that multiple visas would be granted within the body of Christ. At the time I was reflecting, one hundred and seventy-four persons over whom this word was released had received visas. Glory to God!

I was told that a lady travelling by bus to the US embassy was informed that she was sitting in the seat in which I travelled to Kingston on Wednesday nights. The driver of the bus testified that everybody who sat in that seat on their way to the US embassy received their visas. Hallelujah! Do not let that surprise you. These are but a few of the reports of the faithfulness of God in honouring the words which He speaks through His servant.

The Lord has a word for you too! It is not necessarily for the beginning of a new calendar year. At whatever point in time God releases a word over your life, that is a new season; a new day; a new moment. Receive His word in faith, obey His instructions and watch His awesome power transform your life and situation. He did it for me and without fail, He will do it for you.

The word the Lord gave me for His people for the year 2015 came from Job 20:15 and still resonates with me today:

He hath swallowed down riches, and he shall vomit them up again; God shall cast them out of his belly.

At the end of 2014, the Lord said to me, "Son the word for 2015 is that the church should punch the devil in the belly until he vomits up what rightfully belongs to them."

Regrettably, even as the year drew to a close, many had not yet received their blessings. I encouraged them to continue believing that their miracle is still possible because we serve a God who has the power to turn back the hands of time. Don't lose hope, you can still experience restoration. Hallelujah!

The following year, as we stood on the threshold of the year 2016, the Lord spoke to me once more. He said, "Son, 2016, (20 and 16) is made up of the doubling of two numbers-ten and eight." Remember I told you that numbers are significant to God? He reminded me that ten is the number of judgment and plagues and eight is the number of new beginnings. The Lord revealed to me that He was getting ready to use the judgment released on the enemies to bring deliverance to His people.

I reasoned with God and enquired of Him, just how this would be done. The Lord told me that He was about to turn up the heat on the enemies. I was instructed to declare the year 'A YEAR OF WAR!' God was about to war the enemies of His people. He said, "Son, six is the number of creation and I want to do something supernatural in the life of mankind. I want to RECREATE man in the year 2016."

God placed St John 4:6,18 in my spirit for His people:

Now Jacob's well was there. Jesus therefore, being wearied with His journey, sat thus on the well: and it was about the sixth hour.

For thou hast had five husbands; and he whom thou now hast is not thy husband: in that saidst thou truly.

This woman whom Jesus met at the well at the sixth hour was in a relationship with man number six. Let me remind you again, numbers are significant to God and six is the number of man.

Like this woman, your life may be in a mess right now, but God will turn that mess of yours into a message. I am living proof of that.

That is one of the reasons God had me open my life to you in this book. By now you would realize that God has taken me from the ghetto. Just look at me now! I have been placed into His kingdom. I am royalty! Praise God!

Hallelujah! I know who I am! I now declare boldly that where I come from does not define me.

My story is meant to be a catalyst for God to move in the lives of His people as miraculously as He did in mine. You too can know who you are and whose you are. You too can discover the 'dunamis' -strength, power or ability- residing in your belly through the Holy Ghost. My past does not define me. People do not define me either.

I know who I was according to 1 Peter 2:10:

Which in time past were not a people, but are now the people of God: which had not obtained mercy, but now have obtained mercy.

But the most important thing is that I am what God says I am in 1 Peter 2:9:

But ye are a chosen generation, a royal priesthood, an holy nation, a peculiar people; that ye should shew forth the praises of Him who hath called you out of darkness into His marvellous light.

My lifestyle is characterized by this knowledge. I represent the kingdom of our Lord and Saviour Jesus Christ and I endeavour to do it well! People sometimes speak evil of me because of the few material things that God has made me a steward of. I flatly refuse to be offended in the least because I know who I am. I am merely the glory of God on display.

Neither am I perturbed by the enemies. Let them take up their grievances with God. Don't lose focus! Don't be distracted by naysayers. I want every true believer and worshipper to get this message. Don't miss this! I am about to release the key to being blessed in the kingdom of God.

My life is an example of what God can and wants to do in your life today. My God will turn your mess into a message. He specializes in things that appear to be impossible. I love that about my God!

There are three patriarchs by whose names we always refer to our God: The God of Abraham, the God of Isaac and the God of Jacob. One might question why? I believe that it was because God stepped into their mess and turned it into a message.

Abraham was in a mess that appeared to have been impossible for him to escape. He lived this way for seventy-five years. No doubt, at this point it appeared as if all doors were closed. And in fact, they were, by human comprehension.

My God waited until Abraham was seventy-five years old and his wife sixty-five years old. Sarah's biological clock had stopped ticking and Abraham's flesh was dead! A hopeless case, we all agree; but God showed up at that very point and spoke a word over Abraham's life and gave Him an instruction.

In Genesis 12:1-3:

> *Now the LORD had said unto Abram,*
> *Get thee out of thy country, and from thy*
> *kindred, and from thy father's house, unto a*
> *land that I will shew thee:*
> *And I will make of thee a great nation,*
> *and I will bless thee, and make thy name*
> *great; and thou shalt be a blessing;*
> *And I will bless them that bless thee, and*
> *I will curse them that curseth thee; and in*
> *thee shall all families of the earth be blessed.*

God was all too aware of Abraham's embarrassing situation and said to him, "I know that the people around you are laughing you to scorn. I know those in your household consider you as nobody. I know it is disgraceful that at age seventy-five you have produced no seed to ensure the longevity of your father Terah's generation. I know they say that you are an old man. But I am going to raise you up and make your name great."

I know many of you are living among family members and are facing financial embarrassment. God says that He is going to give you houses that you did not build, businesses which you did not start and He is going to make your name known.

Later, in Genesis 14:19-20 Melchizedek, King of Salem and priest of El-Elyon-the Most High God, confirmed God's word to Abraham as the priest blessed him and said:

> *Blessed be Abram of the Most High God,*
> *possessor of heaven and earth:*
> *And blessed be the Most High God, which*
> *hath delivered thine enemies into thy hand.*
> *And he gave him tithes of all.*

In the ensuing chapter, Abram -for that was his name before God changed it- had an awesome encounter with God. His intrinsic motivation to intimately know God drove him to question God about his future. That does not intimidate God. On the contrary, He is attracted to persons who pursue Him passionately.

Genesis 15:5 chronicles God's response to His servant:

> *And He brought him forth abroad, and*
> *said, Look now toward heaven, and tell the*
> *stars, if thou be able to number them: and*
> *He said unto him, So shall thy seed be.*

God said it! Abraham believed it! That settled it! ***And God counted it to him for righteousness*** according to Genesis 15:6

God never fails! Sit tight because God is going to show up in your situation in a supernatural way too. Your mess shall be turned into a message. Do you have any idea who God is? He never fails! The word released from His mouth can never return unto Him without accomplishing that which it was sent to do. Hallelujah!

If God releases a word over your life, I do not care who hates you. Their hatred cannot nullify the word of God. That word must come to pass regardless of how weak or poor you are. All you must do is believe the word and obey God's instructions to you. Yes! Believe it and leave it, for that settles it!

I am speaking directly to a WORRIER! Yes, you! God says to tell you to leave it in His capable hands and begin to worship. Hallelujah! Yes! Go ahead and give God praise! Hallelujah! Hallelujah!

I am a living testimony that God specializes in the things that are impossible with men. Several persons, including my family members, get very emotional, even to the point of tears. This happens whenever they reflect on my past and observe what God is doing presently. It appeared impossible! But God!

How messed up you are today, is of no relevance to me. The greater the mess, the greater the glory of God that will be revealed as your mess is transformed into a message. That is the power of Almighty God on full display.

Allow me to talk to you about the God of Abraham. He, as I said earlier, was in a dark place when God visited Him. Remember that he was told that as the stars are innumerable, so will be his seed? Like most of us, Abraham wanted to know how God was going to fulfil this word. God was not intimidated by his curiosity.

He is God all by Himself! Whether we acknowledge Him or not, He remains Omnipotent, Omnipresent and

Omniscient. Know how to prove your God. Whenever He speaks to you, believe Him. No devil in hell can stop God from showing up in your life. If He showed up for Abraham and for me, I know He will show up for you.

God is about to show up in somebody's life. As I lay in the presence of the Lord one day, as other times, He communed with me. The Lord said, "Son, I've heard you preach that I do not bless mess, where did you get that from?" I replied, "I have heard it preached repeatedly, it sounded good, so I have been preaching it too." The Lord further enquired of me, "Did I tell you that?" By now, I was a bit embarrassed but had to admit that He did not. God said, "Well, son, that is the opposite of what I do. Whenever I see a mess, I want to get into it and turn it into a message. This year it is exactly what I am going to do."

That messy relationship that you are in, God is about to step right into it and recreate your life. There are some drug addicts, scammers, prostitutes and murderers who are crying out, desperately desiring a change. God says to tell you that he has heard your cries and is about to step into your messed up lives. He is about to turn your mess into a message. This is your year! This is your moment! This is your season for a paradigm shift.

He is speaking to that person who is addicted to alcohol, as well as that one hooked on marijuana. You who have been trying to kick the habit of smoking without success, this is your moment! This is the year of deliverance, recreation, and new birth! "It is time!" says the Lord. Now is the time to take that mess and give you a message.

According to the Bible, the woman at the well of Sychar whose name was not even noteworthy, already had five husbands. Her life was indeed messy because she had proceeded to live with man number six. Much to her shame, he was not even hers.

Glory be to God! She met man number seven -Jesus Christ of Nazareth-. He stepped right into her mess and said to her, "I know your life is a mess but I have something special to give you today. Here! Take this water. After drinking it, your life will never be the same."

Are you frustrated with your current situation? God says to tell you that this is the year that He is going to show up in that situation and make your enemies your footstool. This is the year He is removing you from the mire and He is placing you on the choir. This is the year God is relocating you from that pit and positioning you in the pulpit. This is the year God is redeeming you from condemnation and redirecting your life to the congregation. Yes! This is the year for the recreation of your life. He is shifting you from the 'guttermost' and relocating you to the uttermost.

Oh yes! I know that some of the folks around you treat you as if you are nothing because you are in the pit. Go ahead! Let them know, "I am in, but I am on my way out!

I am down, but I am on my way up! God is taking me out! God is lifting me up!"

Go ahead and declare it without fear. No devil in hell can stop you. Open your mouth and boldly declare that this is my year! This is the year for my deliverance! This is the year for my breakthrough! Yes Lord! Yes Jesus! This is the year I have been waiting for! Hallelujah!

God says that He is about to turn that thing right around! Glory to God! Believers, change your position right now. Jump to your feet and make a 360-degree turn. Declare it in the atmosphere, "It's turning around for me! It's turning around for me!" Come on believers, open your mouth! I said to open your mouth and begin to praise God for turning it around right now. Come on and praise your way out of your situation.

Someone is presently paying rent, but God says that this is the year that you will own your own house. Praise your way out of the rented house and praise your way into your own house.

Who am I talking to?

Where is the woman at the well?

I declare to you today that according to your faith, so be it unto you. God is about to recreate your life. God is about to transform your situation. He is about to take that mess and give you a message. You shall run back to all those witchcraft workers and tell them, "Come see a man!"

This is the year that God is going to drop the mouths of all your haters. This is the season of elevation! Open your mouth and praise Him! Magnify the King of kings! If this is for you, exalt your Maker! Worship your Deliverer! Shabach your Way Maker!

Hallelujah! Glory to God! He deserves it! Whenever the praises go up, the blessings come down. It is time to say goodbye to the past years with the mess. Say "Hello!" to your new year and welcome your new season.

To every mess you fell into, say, "Bye bye!" Let every ditch into which you fell know that they are behind you. The past is past! It is time to press into God's presence and experience the present and future that He has for your life.

Go right ahead and close the door to the past. It is behind you, so just forget about the spilt milk. This is a new season! Today is a new day! It is a new year! Happy New Year!

It's time to pray, "Lord, I need a new anointing! I need fresh fire to deal with the fresh set of devils and demons assigned against this new era in my life. Lord, hide me under Your wings. Oh Jesus, please give me comprehensive blood coverage in this season. Keep me in Your secret place, Oh God, in Jesus' name, Amen."

God's people have been plagued for way too long by the demon of poverty and lack. God wants to give you a testimony. I recall a sister who was indebted over three million dollars. I prayed for her, saying, "Lord before the year comes to an end, I am asking you to miraculously cancel that debt."

Just three days before the year ended, she testified that she received the good news that the debt was completely settled. I feel the same anointing is about to be released on someone who is in a similar situation right now. If that's you, go ahead and believe God. Claim the victory and give God thanks for your miracle.

As I am led by the Holy Spirit, I instruct my congregation to sow at different times. One such time is the beginning of the year. I encourage them to present their first fruit to the Lord at this particular time. From Adam to the close of the Bible, no one went before God without an offering. Every patriarch, prophet and king brought an offering each time they came before the Lord. Do not be misled now, whatsoever you sow that is what you are going to reap.

Please pay careful attention as I share with you the principles of how to prosper in the kingdom of God. Many are desirous of knowing the mystery to my being blessed. Here, I give you the key.

In creation, everything yielding fruit carried its seed in itself. Every harvest is therefore wrapped up in a seed. In Genesis 1:11-12:

God said, Let the earth bring forth grass,
the herb yielding seed, and the fruit tree

yielding fruit after his kind, whose seed is in itself, upon the earth; and it was so.

After the flood of the antediluvian world, God made this proclamation in Genesis 8:22:

While the earth remaineth, seedtime and harvest, and cold and heat, and summer and winter, and day and night shall not cease.

The principle of sowing and reaping is a God-ordained one. According to His word, it is operational as long as the earth remains. It is a law which cannot be nullified regardless of our opinions. Of equal importance is the fact that the harvest is wrapped up in the seed.

Now, there is a seed for everything. Contrary to what many believe, prayer is not the seed for wealth, and neither is fasting. Had that been the truth, so many prayer warriors, intercessors and praying church mothers would not have lived such impoverished lives.

If there was not a missing ingredient, they would have prospered in material things as their souls prospered. Sadly, because of ignorance, many lived and died 'as poor as a church mouse'. This happened even though they were totally committed to prayer and fasting.

Why?

I know that you are eager to hear. The answer is quite simple! Anything you sow, that is what you are going to reap. Everything has its seed, including wealth. Here is an example of what I am talking about. A very common complaint from church folks is that there is no love in the church. The principle is the same concerning love- **Whatsoever you sow, that shall you also reap**. So, do you need more love within the body of Christ? If your answer is, "Yes!" Well, all you need to do is sow more love.

Even God, the One who established this principle, obeys it. That is the ultimate reason for entering the earth realm to execute His plan of redemption. God wanted sons on earth, and guess what He did? He first sowed His only begotten Son, Jesus Christ. Speaking of Himself, Jesus said:

> *Except a corn of wheat fall into the ground and die, it abideth alone: but if it dies, it bringeth forth much fruit - John 12:24.*

> *Let us look at Father Abraham of whom we speak so much. We often even sing of him in Sunday school:*

Father Abraham has many sons; many sons have Father Abraham; I am one of them and so are you so let us praise the Lord.

I love that little song. It is one of my favourites. Well, as most persons are aware, when God chose Abraham to be the father of many nations, He instructed him to plant a seed by sacrificing Isaac. He was the very seed through which Abraham anticipated becoming the father of many nations.

In Genesis 22:2, God gave Abraham this instruction:

> *And He said, Take now thy son, thine only son Isaac, whom thou lovest, and get thee into the land of Moriah; and offer him there for a burnt offering upon one of the mountains which I will tell thee of.*

You might also recall that Abraham obeyed the command of the Lord, took his only beloved son, placed him on the altar and raised the knife to slay him. In raising that knife, Abraham had already sacrificed Isaac in his heart.

God stepped in and hindered him from completing the act physically. The scriptures reveal that God honoured Abraham's obedience.

> *Genesis 22:12: And He said, Lay not thine hand upon the lad, neither do thou anything unto him; for now I know that thou fearest God, seeing thou hast not withheld thy son, thine only son from Me.*

Abraham planted a seed and God said in Genesis 22:16-17:

> *By Myself have I sworn, saith the Lord,
> for because thou hast done this thing, and
> hast not withheld thy son, thine only son:
> That in blessing I will bless thee, and in
> multiplying I will multiply thy seed as the
> stars of the heaven, and as the sand which is
> upon the sea shore; and thy seed shall possess
> the gate of his enemies.*

Now this is what blows my mind. Abraham decided to name the place Jehovah Jireh. I asked, "Lord, Jehovah Jireh?" The Lord said, "Yes, Jehovah Jireh." To this point, I was only aware of the popular interpretation of those words-The Lord our provider.

I embarked on a research and discovered that the word 'Jireh' actually means 'sees'. Hence Abraham was saying, "Jehovah sees my giving! He sees my offering! He sees that I gave out of my heart." And it moved God! That right there is a very powerful revelation. I hope you have received it.

Many people covet the little blessings of God on my life. They speak all manner of evil about me to belittle me and defame my character and reputation. According to these haters, preachers should not drive high-end vehicles or live in mansions. They are upset because a faithful God, releases a bountiful harvest.

Where were they when I was planting my seed? They have no idea that in 2003, I had obeyed God's voice and given away my lovely purple Honda Integra. It was just a seed! As you imagine, I questioned God at first. Why would He make such a great demand of me?

To console myself, I reasoned that maybe the Lord doesn't want this car to be a hindrance to my spiritual growth and development. Eventually, I obeyed the voice of God. I did not even get the explanation I sought from Him as to why I was to dispose of it. So, I simply told someone to take it. Years after, God miraculously blessed me with a few high-end vehicles, just like that! Hallelujah!

When Abraham placed Isaac on that altar, God 'saw' and knew that Abraham gave out of the abundance of his heart, not coveting the sacrifice. Beloved, God loveth a cheerful giver (2 Corinthians 9:7). This truth being delivered from the pulpit displeases many people who believe that it is just a gimmick to get people's money.

Regardless, I am still going to give you the key to being blessed. I do so both when I am writing and when I am preaching. God wants you to get this principle and practice it. After you have obeyed, continue to praise and worship Him, while you await your harvest. He has an undisputed track record of being faithful to His word. You shall be blessed!

I am reiterating that this message is from the Lord and is a principle that God established and Himself obeyed. It has not changed! God wants you to give a sacrificial seed for that harvest you desire to reap. Avoid the temptation to be stingy with God. Usually when God asks for a seed, it is the very thing that He wants to bless you with, but better.

If God ever places it in your heart to bless someone with money, usually He wants to bless you with money. If God touches your heart to bless someone with clothes, you can rest assured that you will not be naked. For certain, after you have obeyed and sowed, a harvest of clothing will be released into your life. Nothing is too much to give. Not if God requires it of you. God really wants to bless you.

I say repeatedly that God is going to bless me with houses which I did not build. Many persons ask, "What makes you so certain of this?" My answer is simply this: I have been sowing seeds of houses in the lives of others and according to God's principle, a harvest is certain.

As you by now know, my sister Sonia constantly pours into my life financially and otherwise. Years ago, I received some money from her. She instructed me to purchase a house for myself. No sooner than I put the money aside, the Lord showed me someone in need of a house. God told me that the money I received is a seed for my house, so I should sow it in that individual's life.

Guess what? I obeyed! Yes, I bought the house and delivered it to the child of God. My harvest from that seed is here now! I do not serve money. On the contrary, money serves me. For you are either a servant of money or money is your servant.

Which is it for you?

How do you establish whether you are serving the true and living God or money? Who or what is your God?

There is a money test. If you fail it, God will not entrust you with the blessings He wants to release in your life. You are wondering, "What is the money test?' It is the set of instructions that God has given you to sow financially into a ministry or someone's life. Many people fail almost immediately by issuing a rebuke to the voice of God. 'The blood of Jesus!' **or** 'A di devil a talk to mi!' are common responses to these instructions from God.

As with Abraham, God tests us to determine if He can release that which He has in store for us. This could determine when it is our season. God is saying that He wants to release wealth into the hands of His people. Wealth is what God has in store for us.

This is not for those who are resentful in their hearts whenever God is speaking in this manner. I cannot question the faithfulness of God to honour His spoken word. You see, my life is a testimony to that fact! I speak not only with confidence but with authority.

John the Beloved puts it this way:

> *Beloved, I wish above all things that thou mayest prosper and be in health, even as thy soul prospereth. 3 John:2*

God desires that His people live balanced lives. Being spiritual is first and foremost. Nonetheless, it is well pleasing to God to bless us with sumptuous meals, lovely houses, families and vehicles too. God wants to bless His people! Anything contrary is a lie from the devil. Do not believe it!

The Lord wants you to multiply. Has He promised you anything? As He was faithful to His word to Abraham, so too He will be faithful to all who walk by faith and not by sight. He said, "Blessing, I am going to bless you and multiplying, I am going to multiply you." After all, you are Abraham's seed!

As I was about to conclude this book, the Spirit of the Lord instructed me to sow a seed of seven hundred thousand dollars in someone's life. I obeyed! This is something that I have learnt as a kingdom citizen, I must receive and give freely because God is my source.

Within three weeks of planting that seed, the Lord released another harvest in my life. He upgraded the Toyota vehicle I was driving to a Mercedes Benz. You might think otherwise, but these are ministry tools.

So why do I need them? I don't! But God has chosen to use them to show the ghetto youths that if we honour Him, He will bless us. Confession is good for the soul! Truthfully, I was scared to accept God's blessings initially. I soon realized that this too is a test. The test here is, "Can you stand to be blessed?"

I am rather humbled to be found worthy by God to be entrusted with such a mandate. Thank God for those who continue to pray for me. I too remain prayerful and seek

God's face in fasting, while staying in the word. With each blessing, I become hungrier for the requisite wisdom, knowledge and understanding to be a good and faithful steward.

As a servant of God, I am all too aware of my responsibilities to my children, other blood relatives, church family and fellowmen. I desire that by God's grace and mercy, I will release the life-transforming message of the Kingdom of God. I must also reveal the key to prosperity in God's Kingdom. To effect change in the lives of people as I am led by the Spirit of God, is my ultimate goal.

Who is the richest man to have graced the face of this earth? The Bible ascribes this accomplishment to King Solomon. However, it is important to scrutinize his life to ascertain how he managed to amass such wealth. I want to assist you with that as I give to you the key to being blessed as citizens of God's Kingdom.

It was customary in Israel for kings to sacrifice to Jehovah God. Solomon adhered to the custom but did something no one before or after him ever did. That thing drew His God's attention. Do you want to get out of poverty? Do it like Solomon! Do you want your present situation to be turned around? Do it like Solomon!

I am taking my time to teach you this principle. It is the key to receiving that breakthrough you so desperately need. In the same manner which God revealed it to me, I am delivering it to you. My hope and trust is that it will be received in faith and your life will become a testimony.

God is looking for messy lives to transform in the same way that He did mine. Wisdom is the ability to identify differences. I repeat, wisdom is the ability to identify differences. This includes differences in people as well as in the atmosphere.

A wise person is, therefore, able to detect whenever they are in an atmosphere of wealth. Whenever you do, seize the opportunity to get God's attention with your sacrificial giving. Once you have obeyed God, it is time to praise your way into your harvest.

When it was Solomon's time to sacrifice, they came with a bullock, but he said, "Stop! I cannot give God just one bullock. My God deserves much more than that." Someone might have suggested that ten should be enough. Solomon disagreed with that suggestion too.

No one expected him to refute a recommendation to sacrifice one hundred bullocks. But he did! Solomon was determined to out-give every king who preceded him. He dared to conceive the thought that he could actually outgive God. This was not being disrespectful; he was just being grateful! Solomon said, "I know that one bullock is the standard requirement, but my God deserves so much more than that. I am giving one thousand bullocks." And he did!

I want to draw the attention of the stingy folks who are expecting great blessings from God. A change of mentality is what I hope to help you develop so that you can be blessed by God. Do you know that some Christians murmur and complain whenever there is an opportunity for them to give sacrificially? These same people are usually moved to envy when sinners obey God's principles and receive His blessings.

This is more than just a principle; it is a universal law. I repeat, it is a universal law:

> *Whatsoever a man sows that shall ye also reap. Galatians 6:7*

You are in an atmosphere to receive wisdom so stick with me and learn. It is almost the end of the journey on which you have embarked to read this book. It would be rather disappointing if you were to disembark at this moment. All that you have read of my personal life is meaningless if you do not get what I am imparting at this juncture. God wants to bless you. Let me show you how.

God is a God of reciprocity! At the end of Solomon's sacrificing, he had a divine visitation. In that encounter, God asked Solomon what he desired in return for such great sacrifice.

God said, Ask what I shall give thee in 1 Kings 3:5

Solomon requested an understanding heart. However, God said that He reciprocates with multiplication. So, instead of granting King Solomon's request, God added that which Solomon did not ask for - riches and honour-

. My God! Solomon could not out-give God! Neither can you.

Once again, Solomon sought to out-give God when the ark of the Lord was being brought back into the Most Holy place. Here he sacrificed sheep and oxen that could not be numbered for multitude as recorded in 1Kings 8:6. At the end of this exercise, God again visited Solomon. My! My! Do you realize that sacrifice gets God's attention?

This time the Shekinah Glory of Almighty God, in the form of a cloud, filled the House of the Lord. The glory of the Lord was such that the priests could not stand to minister. Solomon supplicated before God for the people in his prayer as he dedicated the temple. He then went on to sacrifice twenty-two thousand oxen and one hundred and twenty thousand sheep in the dedication ceremony.

In 1Kings 8:64 we are told:

> *The king hallowed the middle of the court that was before the house of the Lord; for there he offered burnt offerings and meat offerings: because the brazen altar that was before the LORD was too little to receive the burnt offerings, and the meat offerings and the fat of the peace offerings.*

Maybe this time Solomon thought that surely, he had out-given both man and God. To his surprise, after this mammoth exercise, the LORD visited him again. God acknowledged the petition he made and established the conditions under which He would bless the people. You can find the details in 1Kings 9:1-9. No one can out-give God!

> *Give, and it shall be given unto you; good measure, pressed down, and shaken together, and running over, shall men give into your bosom. For with the same measure that ye mete withal it shall be measured to you again. Luke 6:38*

Solomon himself left us with keys to being prosperous in Ecclesiastes 11:1,4 and 6:

> *Cast thy bread upon the waters: for thou shalt find it after many days.*
> *He that observeth the wind shall not sow; and he that regardeth the clouds shall not reap.*
> *In the morning sow thy seed, and in the evening withhold not thine hand: for thou knowest not whether shall prosper, either this or that, or whether they both shall be alike good.*

Should you find it challenging to take advice from me; there you have it from the wisest man. Those instructions confirm all that I have been trying to share. If you want to be blessed, you must give! The harvest you will reap is directly related to the seed which you sow.

Having obeyed the principle, I am sharing with you, I am unstoppable! I tell people all the time that "No obeah can stop me! Dem coulda go a Haiti, ninety or hundred fi mi nuh cum to nutten ina life! Dem only a waste dem time an money." That was a local colloquialism with which you might be unfamiliar. I will repeat the message in Standard English: "No witchcraft can stop me! Wherever they choose to go to have witchcraft done, that will not hinder me from succeeding in life; they are wasting their time and money."

Why? Because I know how to move God and whom God blesses no man can curse - Numbers 23:8. People of God, true worshippers, God says to tell you:

> *Give, and it shall be given unto you; good measure, pressed down, and shaken together, and running over, shall men give into your bosom.*

Some devils are holding up wealth with your name on it and God wants to release it. I know this topic creates much tension, so some of you have been enjoying the book to this point, but you are now becoming tense and uncomfortable. However, the truth is, if you are having that experience, it is an indication that I am touching your god (money).

Those who worship money are offended when I touch their god but I still have a God-given responsibility to tell you the truth. **IF YOU WANT IT, YOU HAVE TO PLANT IT!** Did you get that? Ok, I will repeat, **IF YOU WANT IT, YOU HAVE TO PLANT IT!** And whatsoever you plant, that is certainly what you are going to reap.

Equally important is the need to check your attitude towards planting. God loveth a cheerful giver.

If you sow sparingly, you shall reap sparingly and if you sow bountifully, you shall reap bountifully. 2 Corinthians 9:6.

This is for the reader who is anticipating a turn-around in this season of your life. In order to reap it, you must plant it. Solomon, the wisest man implored us to keep planting. Even if you have already planted six or seven times, do not be afraid to plant the eighth time.

Who knows, the first or second seed you planted may have been devoured by the cankerworm. However, if numerous seeds are continuously planted in fertile soil, you must eventually reap a harvest. Solomon also encouraged us to cast our bread upon the waters and we shall find it after many days.

The door is open for disappointment to walk in whenever we anticipate a harvest tomorrow from the seed sown today. Some seeds which are planted today will not produce a harvest for us but for our grand and great-grandchildren. Yes! Some harvests are reserved for their college and university tuition. The Omniscient God knows that they will need it in the future. In His wisdom, He holds back the harvest from you and stores it up for them. Imagine how awful you would feel being aged and unable to assist them, even though you have a strong desire to see them succeed.

Our God is so amazing! As your offspring embarks on their tertiary level of academic development, God just moves the heart of a complete stranger-including sinners. Faithfully, He transfers wealth into the lives of your third and fourth generation; just like that!

That's a harvest from seeds sown years before. God declares that the wealth of the wicked is laid up for the righteous. So that transfer - believe it or not- is a part of His principle. Still in the dark? I hope not, because maybe the only other way for you to receive it is by being in church. In that atmosphere, I could instruct your neighbour to slap you and tell you, "If you want it, you have to plant it!"

A lot has been said and there is still so much more in my spirit that I want to share with you. Let us pause for a moment and reflect on the writings in the Old Testament. Have you observed the different offerings that were sacrificed to the Lord?

It would be beneficial to invest some time in studying Deuteronomy and Leviticus. You would be surprised to discover that so many sacrifices were made. Yet you have been familiar with only one or two. There is the sin offering, heave offering, trespass offering, grain offering, drink offering, meat offering, burnt offering and freewill offering.

Different offerings moved God in different ways. Most of us are only accustomed to the freewill offering and the devil has used its definition to trick many of us. A common practice is to give the coins or the smallest, most wrinkled notes as a freewill offering. We have been conditioned to give the worst and least to God when He is expecting us to give our best.

God is not moved by anything less than our best. We might say, "It is of my own free will so this is what I am giving." That is true! No one should force you to do otherwise. Rest assured though, that unless God is moved by your giving, you will never be blessed.

Abraham, Isaac, Jacob and Moses all used their offerings to move God. However, Solomon, being wiser, gave extraordinarily and abundantly above all that they sacrificed to the Lord before him. He also raised the bar in his giving so high that it remains unchallenged and unmatched today.

How is your giving? This is a good time to check. See if you are giving your best to God because I am about to release a life-changing word from the Lord.

Some time ago, a group of people conspired and stole some equipment from our church. What they were ignorant of, is the fact that their actions were tantamount to sowing seeds. Their harvest is sure! Their actions opened the door for the devourer to steal from them as they stole from the church.

More importantly, however, was the fact that years before being placed over the flock of King Jesus Pentecostal Fellowship, the Lord had moved me to sow. At His command, I used all my savings to bless the church I was attending with some much-needed equipment.

Little had I known that the very moment that our equipment was stolen, the Lord would release a harvest from that seed. It had been sown years before. Back then, I was little Brother Baker in a small board structure. In less than two weeks after the incident, the Lord blessed us to the overflowing. We were able to replace that which was stolen with much better equipment.

We also took the opportunity to sow equipment into other ministry points and still had equipment in reserve. What a harvest! The devil's decision to touch our equipment was an opportunity for God to open a double door. They thought that they were emptying the church. The fact is that they paved the way for us to receive more than what we needed and of much better quality too.

If you have sown good seeds in fertile soil and the cankerworm devoured them or the thief broke in and stole them, this is your season. God is going to command the enemy to restore four times what was taken. Hallelujah! Jehovah Jireh! Jehovah Jireh!

Chapter 14

Unlocking The Blessings

I speak over your life and that of your loved ones this very moment. We speak to you ………… (name the day, month, year, season) OPEN! In the name of Jesus Christ of Nazareth. OPEN! OPEN! OPEN!

At the beginning of the year 2015, the Lord instructed me through the Holy Ghost to give Him the very first money that I received from His people. In obedience, I released the seed of the believers' first fruit into the work of the Lord. I was determined that I would use none of it to meet even my basic needs. God has since given me a hundredfold harvest and continues to bless me.

Now it is your opportunity to use the key I have given you and to watch God manifest His power. I challenge you to obey and let Him give you a mind-blowing harvest. In the seed is everything you need! Listen and obey the voice of God as He moves you to sow into someone's life or a ministry.

Be sure to give what you have been instructed to give! Resist any temptation to give what you desire to give. If you obey the Spirit of God, Jehovah Jireh will honour His word to you.

Abraham, we are told, is the father of faith and of them that believe. The word of God declares that as many as carry the faith of Abraham are blessed with faithful Abraham. On every occasion that Abraham presented himself before God, he carried an offering.

In sharing with you the various offerings given to the Lord in the Old Testament records, I deliberately omitted the 'wave offering'. I reserved its mention for this moment. It is common practice for congregants to be instructed to give the Lord a wave offering. At such prompting, persons would lift their hands and wave them before the Lord.

That is not really a wave offering. The wave offering; sheaf offering; omer offering was an offering made by the Jewish priests in token of a solemn special presentation to God (Exodus 29:24, 26, 27; Leviticus 7:34; 8:27; 9:21; 10:14, 15). The sheaf, omer or wave-offering then became the property of the priest.

In Leviticus 23:9-20 the Lord gave Moses this instruction which explains what a wave offering is:

> *Speak unto the children of Israel, and say unto them, When ye be come into the land which I give unto you, and shall reap the harvest thereof, then ye shall bring a sheaf of the first fruits of your harvest unto the priest.*
>
> *And he shall wave the sheaf before the LORD, to be accepted for you: on the*

morrow after the Sabbath the priest shall wave it.

And ye shall offer that day when ye wave the sheaf and the lamb without blemish of the first year for a burnt offering unto the LORD.

And the meat offering thereof shall be two tenth deals of fine flour mingled with oil, an offering made by fire unto the LORD for a sweet savour: and the drink offering thereof shall be of wine, the fourth part of an hin.

And ye shall eat neither bread, nor parched corn, nor green ears, until the selfsame day that ye have brought an offering unto your God: it shall be a statute forever throughout your generations in all your dwellings.

And ye shall count unto you from the morrow after the Sabbath, from the day that ye brought the sheaf of the wave offering; seven Sabbaths shall be complete:

Even unto the morrow after the seventh Sabbath shall ye number fifty days; and ye shall offer a new meat offering unto the LORD.

Ye shall bring out of your habitations two wave loaves of two tenth deals: they shall be fine flour; they shall be baken with leaven; they are the firstfruits unto the LORD.

> *And ye shall offer with bread seven lambs without blemish of the first year, and one young bullock, and two rams: they shall be for a burnt offering unto the LORD, with their meat offering, and their drink offerings, even an offering made by fire, of sweet savour unto the LORD.*
>
> *Then ye shall sacrifice one kid of the goats for a sin offering, and two lambs of the first year for a sacrifice of peace offerings.*
>
> *And the priest shall wave them with the bread of the firstfruits for a wave offering before the LORD, with the two lambs, they shall be holy unto the LORD for the priest.*

Abraham brought his beloved son Isaac and placed him before the Lord -the first-fruit of the children of promise-. Similarly, the children of Israel brought the first fruits of their increase and waved it before the Lord in obedience to His command. This would not only be indicative of their obedience but also their petition to God to accept their offering and bless them in return.

God is a God of reciprocity! I mentioned it earlier. As Abraham waved his sacrifice, giving his best to the Lord with an attitude of gratitude, Jehovah God sent an angel to pronounce a blessing on him.

This message rings out from Genesis throughout the ages. Whether, through Apostle Paul or another servant of God, it was reiterated by the author of the book of

Hebrews. The saints were encouraged to be faithful in their giving. Hebrews 6:12-14 speaks of God's faithfulness and immutability, not only to Abraham but also to us who give as sincerely as he did:

> *That ye be not slothful, but followers of them who through faith and patience inherit the promises.*
>
> *For when God made promise to Abraham, because He could swear by no greater, He swore by Himself, Saying, Surely, blessing I will bless thee, and multiplying I will multiply thee.*
>
> *And so, after he had patiently endured, he obtained the promise.*

This is a new season, a new day, maybe a new month or even a new year. It is the season of change! God is going to turn your situation upside-down! God is about to turn your mess into a message!

Abraham's flesh was dead and Sarah's womb was dead. Nonetheless, because Abraham believed God, the word of God says of him:

> *(As it is written, I have made thee a father of many nations,) before Him whom he believed, even God, who quickeneth the dead and calleth those things which be not as though they were.*

> *Who against hope believed in hope, that he might become the father of many nations; according to that which was spoken, so shall thy seed be.*
>
> *And being not weak in faith, he considered not his own body now dead, when he was an hundred years old, neither yet the deadness of Sara's womb:*
>
> *He staggered not at the promise of God through unbelief; but was strong in faith, giving glory to God;*
>
> *And being fully persuaded that, what He had promised, He was able to perform.*

That's so powerful! Believe that you are the head and not the tail! Believe that you shall lend and not borrow! I encourage you to believe God! Believe God! Believe God! Regardless of the curse that might be on your life, extend your faith and believe God.

I am not deterred by the nature of the curse. Maybe it is generational or otherwise. So, what if no one in your family owns land? What if no one owns a house? None of that can hinder God's word concerning you from being fulfilled. The word from Almighty God is that the curse shall be broken! I dare you to believe God.

I have experienced so much opposition because of where God has taken me from: The Guttermost - to the Uttermost!

The BMX bicycle - to BMW and Mercedes Benz.

Riding in Negril selling ice-cream cake and fudge - to the pulpit.

Being the black sheep in my family - to someone whom my family can be proud to acknowledge.

Having a tainted police record - to an expunged police record.

Being unable to travel overseas - to travelling to numerous countries including the Holy Land- Israel.

Being a nobody - to being somebody.

Being in poverty - to being royalty.

I am now a king and a priest in the Kingdom of God.

Guess what? As soon as God transformed my life, many people turned against me. They included some in my hometown, even church folks. I had so many friends or so I thought. Overseer Terrance Mullings is one of the few who has remained with me. I have known him since we were at Savanna la mar Secondary School.

We slept in the same house, which evolved into a ranch. There was not even a decent bed, but we were grateful that we were sheltered and made ourselves comfortable. Sometimes we were content with even being on the floor.

We made wood fire, cooked and ate together from the same pot. White rice and tin boom (mackerel) was our main dish. Since none of us owned a motor vehicle and we were unable to find money for taxi fares, we begged for rides to go to church.

Unbelievable but true! Some of these same so-called friends saw the blessings of the Lord on my life and began to spread propaganda. They lied that I am demonstrating powers acquired through involvement in witchcraft. Naturally, most people would be gullible to their wicked lies. Bear in mind that these friends -now operating as enemies- are speaking as insiders.

These same Judases witnessed me seeking the Lord earnestly and desperately. They knew that I was determined to see the manifested glory and power of God revealed in my life. At one point, I went into fasting and prayer and eventually went without food for forty-three days. Throughout this wilderness experience, water was all I consumed. There was an inner cry! I hungered and thirsted after righteousness and still do.

Their ultimate goal was to hinder God's plan to elevate me, but Isaiah 54:17 declares otherwise:

> *No weapon that is formed against thee shall prosper; and every tongue that shall rise against thee in judgment thou shalt condemn. This is the heritage of the servants of the LORD, and their righteousness is of Me, saith the Lord.*

I take this scripture quite personally. I have been privileged and humbled to witness many confessions from some of these persons publicly and privately. Some have stood before congregations, while others called my cell phone or visited my home. All done to the glory of God!

I have forgiven, released and blessed them all in prayer as I too continue to need God's forgiveness daily.

I concur with Jeremiah's testimony in Jeremiah 20:11

> *But the LORD is with me as a Mighty Terrible One: therefore my persecutors shall stumble, and they shall not prevail; they shall be greatly ashamed; for they shall not prosper.*

The more they fight, the more God elevates me. I want you to remember that Jehovah sees. He sees your tears! He hears your cries! He sees your affliction and He has come down to deliver you from those wicked mouths. He is here to deliver you from bad-minded Christians and family members. He has given you the power to condemn every wicked and lying tongue that has revolted against you.

God says to tell you that your next offering is a wave offering before Him. It is an offering for the season of life you are entering. As you wave it before Him, pray this simple prayer:

"God, please look on my offering as You looked upon Abraham's, David's and Moses'. Lord, I am planting this seed for the next season of my life and believing that every curse and demonic assignment to block my prosperity is broken in Jesus' name."

Let me join you in praying:

Lord, I pray, please release high-ranking angels to fight for Your people. Oh God! Please release high-ranking angels to fight and deliver us from the hands of the wicked in Jesus' name.

Go ahead and wave your offering before God in faith wherever you are. In the spirit, I hear God rebuking someone right now who is rebellious to the word of the Lord. There is someone who also wants to sow what you feel like sowing and ignore what the Spirit of God instructed you to sow. God is sending you back to your bag, purse, pocket, pocketbook, billfold or cheque-book because of your disobedience.

God is allowing you to tap into what He is about to release upon His people in this new season. God says that this seed shall surely bring forth a harvest. It is going to break that curse in your life. You are going around in a circle long enough. Someone needs a job and this seed is going to move God so that you receive a job that you are not even qualified for. I hear the Holy Ghost saying that before the month ends, you shall receive a job.

Someone with a court case who cannot afford to retain the services of a lawyer, God says that this seed is giving you a lawyer. He says that He shall defend you. Hallelujah!

There is a reader desirous of going to the United States embassy but is unable to secure the funds to do so. God says that He is going to touch your relatives overseas and they are going to send you the money. Hallelujah!

I feel a release! I feel a release! My God! I feel a release right now!

Somebody is living under bondage. Your family continually pushes you around because you are living with them. God says that He is giving you your own house. Glory! Come on! You better believe God! You better believe God! I say that you better believe God! Hallelujah! Holy Spirit! Wave that offering before God. Heaven shall look down on that seed today.

God told me that money is the most flexible seed. You can sow money for healing, a husband, a wife or material. God says that it is a flexible seed because it is your substance. That explains why we are instructed in the word of God to:

> *Honour the LORD with thy substance,*
> *and with the first-fruits of all thine increase:*
> *So shall thy barns be filled with plenty, and*
> *thy presses shall burst out with new wine*
> *(Proverbs 3:9).*

Everyone cannot receive this word from the Lord because many desire to be blessed but are real doubters. If you are reading this message and like Abraham, you believe that God will honour His word, you are positioned for a breakthrough. This section is for believers!

Whenever God wants to bless you, He will not only tell you what to sow but where to sow it. It is important that whoever received this instruction from the Lord, sow your seed with all your heart. You ought to be able to declare truthfully that this seed I am sowing is what God has led me to sow and I am sowing it with all my heart. Most assuredly, you shall receive a testimony. You shall record your miracle and share it with everyone you meet.

I am calling all true believers; all true worshippers; all the praisers who believe God for a miracle! A woman is declaring that the seed she is sowing is for the salvation of her son. God says to tell you that He is going to save him.

Where are the believers? Where are the true worshippers? This is your moment! It is time to get radical! Get the doubt out of your mind and spirit right now and give God the praise He deserves. Hallelujah! Get ready to give God a sacrifice of praise along with that offering you are waving before Him.

A reader experiencing financial difficulties with your mortgage payments; God says to tell you that this seed is fixing that problem.

Someone is undergoing problems with a piece of land. The enemy is determined to take the land from you. Not so! God says that as you wave this seed before Him, He is placing that parcel of land in your hands. Hallelujah!

I declare over your life that this is the year! This is your moment! This is your season! Wave that offering before the Lord. Wherever you are, raise that offering before Almighty God. Go ahead and wave it. Hallelujah! Wherever you are, Jehovah sees! Jehovah sees! Jehovah sees! Hallelujah!

Say, "Look on my offering Oh God; I am giving it from my heart. I am planting it in Your kingdom, Oh God."

God asked the rhetorical question in Malachi 3:8: **_Will a man rob God?_** The answer is an astounding, "Yes!" God says,

> **_"Yet ye have robbed me. But ye say, Wherein have we robbed Thee? In tithes and offerings."_**

God gave you a seed to plant in His kingdom and you ate it instead, thus robbing God. But God wants to reverse the curse and release a blessing into your life. That is why He is giving you another opportunity. This very moment He is saying to someone, "I want you to release that seed from a sincere heart, for I the Lord loveth a cheerful giver."

I feel someone getting ready to release their seed from a genuine heart. The Lord wants someone to develop the right attitude towards giving. He does not want you to miss your moment.

God says that this offering is going to release an overseas connection for someone. This particular person was previously connected and was receiving assistance but the relationship deteriorated and the assistance ceased.

God says that this seed is going to move God and He will, in turn, touch the heart of that individual. "You will receive a telephone call," says the Lord. God says to tell you that whenever this call comes, speak nothing of the past disagreements. Forget it and move forward. Just praise God and be warm and friendly to the individual. God says that this is a door He is reopening for you to be blessed.

Do you believe God? If you do, lift your hand in the air and wave your offering before God. Wave it! I hear God saying that somebody's business is on the verge of collapsing but this seed is going to revive it. This year your business is going to take off.

God says that it is time for a shift! Some Jamaicans are reluctant to support fellow Jamaicans in business. Do not turn your backs on your brothers and sisters who are operating small businesses. The income they receive from your support is being reinvested in our own country and is rebuilding our economy.

There is a sister with a grocery shop or a brother with a hardware store. Their goods might even be more expensive but consider your support a seed being sown into their lives.

According to God's word,

> *"As we have therefore opportunity, let us do good unto all men; especially unto them who are of the household of faith."*

Do not expect to receive the merchandise or service of your brothers and sisters in business for free. Instead, allow them to keep the change you should receive as a seed for the prosperity of their businesses. Encourage others to be supportive of them. With your support and encouragement, their businesses will expand. Sow a seed and let Jehovah see!

Enquire among yourselves for skilled workers and allow them to get the job done. There are dressmakers, tailors, carpenters, masons, cooks, cleaners, mechanics, telephone technicians and the list goes on - utilize their services and support their businesses.

By these actions, you are creating young entrepreneurs. That is wisdom! I just gave you a wisdom key! Support those who are among you in the body of Christ. Be your brother's keeper! Be vigilant! Your desire is for God to bless you. You desire to receive support from others in your endeavours so go ahead and support each other.

Now lift your wave offering to the Lord as I pray this prayer:

Father, in the name of Jesus, here we are before You. It is written in Your word, "Whatsoever a man soweth, that shall ye also reap." Father, we are here at this moment under financial attack. The cankerworm has devoured our grand and great grandparents' wealth. Lord, they sucked the sour grapes and left the teeth of this generation on edge.

Father, in the name of Jesus, we ask You to show up! Please, Father, bind the palmerworm, the cankerworm, the locust and the caterpillar. The wealth which they have eaten up, Father release to us Oh Lord!

Please give us a harvest, not thirtyfold, not sixtyfold but Lord, release a hundredfold in this season; this year!

Father in the name of Jesus Christ I pray right now that You will release high-ranking angels to arrest these demons of lack. Arrest the poverty demons, Oh God and release an overflow in the lives of Your people.

Oh God, You did it for Abraham, Isaac and Jacob. Do it again Holy Spirit so that Your people will praise You with a free heart. So that they will praise You and the world will see that Jehovah provides! That the world may see that Jehovah God is our provider! Hallelujah!

Father, we thank You now for this breakthrough! We thank You for the radical turnaround! We thank You that You are releasing high-ranking angels right now to prepare a table before Your people in the presence of our enemies.

Our enemies shall see Your blessings upon our lives and shall come and praise You. They shall see how You elevate us and surrender to You; worshipping You, our God.

Let them confess that of truth, You are a God who opens doors that no man can shut. Hallelujah!

(Lift that offering before God)

Father, please consume it with Your fire!

Some of the offerings being brought before You have curses on them because the enemy has released these curses to take away the wealth of Your people.

Some of the hands raised before You Oh Lord, they are chained;

Some have ropes; Some have threads which have tied and bound them in poverty Oh God.

But this very moment, I pray that You will release fire Oh God and utterly destroy every curse in the mighty name of Jesus Christ. Hallelujah!

Release the fire of God to burn every demon that holds Your people captive, right now in Jesus' name!

The fire of God shall destroy every witchcraft, every sorcery, every black magic, de Laurence and lodge demons risen up against God's people!

We burn them with fire!

> *The Holy Spirit; the fire of God consumes every net; burns up every arrow and every house that is set to cage Your people!*
>
> *Every prison, the fire of God consumes it! Hallelujah!*

Now go ahead and plant that seed in the kingdom of God according to the direction of the Holy Spirit. As you do, declare these words over your seed: Father I plant this seed in Jesus' name. I plant it in the name of Jesus! Seed, multiplying you shall multiply; Blessing you shall bless! Hallelujah!

God says:

> *By Myself have I sworn, for because thou hast done this thing, and hast not withheld thy son, thine only son:*
>
> *That in blessing I will bless thee, and in multiplying I will multiply thy seed as the stars of the heaven, and as the sand which is upon the sea shore; and thy seed shall possess the gate of his enemies;*
>
> *And in thy seed shall all the nations of the earth be blessed; because thou hast obeyed My voice. (Genesis 22:16-18)*

All who planted this seed shall likewise reap the benefits. Also, God says that because you have sown from your heart, your enemies shall be under your feet. The sole of your feet shall be in the necks of your enemies. All of this is yours because you obeyed the voice of the Lord. Hallelujah!

God is reversing death right now! Some persons are supposed to be diagnosed with cancer this year. You had better believe that God is reversing that right now! Some persons are to be diagnosed with high blood pressure but believe that God is reversing it right now! Some persons are supposed to be diagnosed with diabetes and heart disease. Believe that God is reversing them right now! Some are to die in car accidents but believe that God is reversing that right now!

Today is the first day of a new season in your life and I am declaring and decreeing that God is honouring your sacrifice. Some of you are not really aware of what God is doing but some believers are moved by faith and not by sight.

In the Bible, an incident was chronicled of the collection of the offering in the New Testament. Jesus could have sat at the back or in the middle of the congregation. Instead, He stood and observed everyone's giving. At the end of their giving, Jesus announced that the poor widow who gave the two mites had out-given all the others. That is because she gave all, despite her need.

Some Christians would have advised her to keep it to buy food since it was all she had. But her giving did not go unnoticed and according to God's word in Luke 6:38

Give, and it shall be given unto you; good measure, pressed down, and shaken together, and running over, shall men give into your bosom. For with the same measure that ye mete withal it shall be measured to you again.

I witnessed God honouring the faith of a woman, during a service where the first fruits were being sown. She walked forward in tears and shared this story: "I desired to sow a seed of Two Thousand dollars for the salvation of my son but had only One Thousand dollars. I cried out to the Lord, telling Him my heart's desire. While worshipping, someone held my hand and released something into it. I opened my eyes and looked into my hands and there was a thousand dollar-bill.

Now I could sow the seed I wanted to sow. Brethren who could it be but Jesus?"

I told you that Jehovah sees! This is the most difficult message to deliver. Preachers are afraid to preach about money in the churches. Most people serve the god 'money'. So, whenever their god is being talked about, they are offended. Preachers are cognizant of this fact, so to avoid offending their congregants, they evade the issue.

However, some servants of God carry a cutting-edge anointing. These preachers preach as they are instructed by the Holy Ghost. As for me, whatever God tells me to preach, I am committed to preaching just that - I really do not care!

God warned me a long time ago that if I refused to preach what He instructs me to deliver to the people, He is going to confound me right before their eyes. God said to me, "Son, set your face like flint and preach exactly what I tell you to preach."

That is just what I am committed to doing until death, by God's grace assisting me.

Chapter 15

Can Do Power

I remember just where I was when God visited me. Likewise, He can show up in your situation right now, regardless of where you are and what you are doing.

The devil will do anything to hinder you from reading this book, but the fact that you have got this far is an indication that you can be hindered but you cannot be stopped.

You are unstoppable! Like me, if the devil could have stopped you, your bones would have been white. Yes! You would have been dead! God has been good to us and that is why I invite you to leave whatever you are doing, clap your hands and just give God praise.

Magnify the King; He is worthy and deserves every Hallelujah!

In Philippians 4v13, Paul writing to the church in Philippi said:

> *I can do all things through Christ which strengtheneth me.*

God says to tell you that you can handle it! I know it is rough, but you can handle it! I know it is tough, but you can handle it! I know that hell is released against you, but you can handle it! I know the enemies and the fire 'tun up' against you, but you can handle it!

Come on and encourage yourself and wherever possible, encourage somebody else. Tell someone, "God says that you can handle it!" If you could not, it would not have come your way. The mere fact that it has come is indicative of the fact that you can handle it.

It cannot destroy you! God would never allow it to come your way to destroy you. He, who is faithful and true, has your life penned out. Neither will He go back on the word He has spoken over you. His plan for your life must be accomplished!

It was not your choice to be where you are in life right now; it is God's doing. You did not choose the family that you were born into, God designed it. Just being alive today, is adequate proof that God has endued you with the power to handle whatever you are encountering right now!

You can handle the hypocrites at your workplace. You can handle the boss who wants to demote or dismiss you. Yes, you can handle it! You can handle that cruel neighbour who wants to run you out of town. Yes, you can handle it! God has designed you in such a unique manner. He has deposited resilience in your spirit to successfully manoeuvre the challenging developments along the pathway of your life.

Just the fact that you were placed in your mother's womb and born into that family is adequate proof that God has a plan for you. Whether you are aware of it or not, He has been in control all this time. Regardless of the contrary winds, God's got you!

On your way to destiny, there will be some unexpected problems. Circumstances intended to derail you from fulfilling your destiny will periodically arise. However, I want to assure or reassure you that the God who calls you, the God who made you, never says, "Oops!"

Absolutely nothing takes Him by surprise. Before He made you, He was already in possession of all the intricate details of all the experiences you would have in your entire lifetime. In His infinite wisdom, He placed something inside of your spirit. Otherwise, you would never have survived all that the devil placed on you to this point.

Remember Job? The devil had to get God's permission to touch Him and God set the boundaries that determined in what areas he could be attacked. Therefore, nothing you are presently facing is surprising to God.

God already knew what would surface and at what time it would. The 'Can Do Power' is in you. You shall not, will not and cannot fail.

Chapter 16

The Mandate

For whom He did foreknow, He also did predestinate to be conformed to the image of His Son, that He might be the firstborn among many brethren.

Moreover whom He did predestinate, them He also called: and whom He called, them He also justified: and whom He justified, them He also glorified.

What shall we then say to these things? If God be for us, who can be against us?

He that spared not His own Son, but delivered Him up for us all, how shall He not with Him also freely give us all things? Romans 8:29-32.

I find it impossible to condemn persons because of their background or present condition. Not that I am immune from condemnatory thoughts but I always reflect on my own life. Whenever I do that, the thought of writing off others quickly dissipates.

Recently I went out and bought a bicycle. Somehow, I felt led in my spirit to keep it as a reminder of where the

Lord is taking me from. I am resolute -by God's grace- to allow nothing that God has made me a steward of, to replace Him in my life.

One Saturday at midnight, I lay in bed asking the Lord which vehicle I was to drive to Kingston. I was getting ready to leave out to attend the Sunday morning service which was then held at our head office branch on third Sundays. Immediately, I had a flashback of where the Lord had taken me from. My heart melted within me. I was not only filled with gratitude but overwhelmed. No one will ever understand like I do, the goodness and awesomeness of Daddy Jesus in this little Baker boy's life. His hand on my life simply humbles me.

This is what drives me not only to write my story but to preach. I am propelled by a burning desire to see God do for others what He did for me. I desperately want to see the prostitutes, addicts, convicts, rejects and condemned come to realize that there is a bright future in God. All is made possible through our Lord and Saviour-Jesus Christ.

My mission is to bring hope, help and healing to millions who are lost and dying in this world. Many ask me, "Bishop how do you keep up with such a tight ministry schedule?" My response is, "Jesus!" It is the Christ in me that energizes me so I can accomplish the mission.

I cannot help but preach! In a recent conversation with some of my brethren, I was reminded of some of the moments that blew their minds. They rehearsed the events of the afternoon when I went to play football with the youths in my community. On this occasion, I went to the Savanna-la-mar Primary School's playfield.

An accident resulted in my receiving a laceration on my bottom lip. Oh my, it bled profusely! It was a service night, so immediately after I got medical attention, I headed to church. It was my intention to relax so that the bandage would remain in place. I also wanted to avoid any resumption of bleeding.

Guess what? I sat on the rostrum until I was asked to say something to reassure concerned members of the congregation that I was doing ok. It turned out that I preached the bandage off! God got the glory, but the wound began bleeding once more.

I was rushed back to the doctor, treated once again and sent home. Some think this is ridiculous; others say it is foolish. But the fire in me just won't go out. For me, preaching is innate! I was born again with it! Please pray for me!

On another occasion, I was having an extremely high fever accompanied by weakness. It was a Tuesday night; the night on which the weekly street meetings were held in the parish capital. Somehow, I made it to the vehicle and drove to the location. I instructed Overseer Mullings on how to organize the meeting so that I would not have to preach.

As the meeting progressed, I gained enough strength to scramble to the area reserved for me and sat. Like a mantle, I felt the anointing envelope me, as the time came for the preaching of the word. Unctioned to function, I took the microphone and preached as I was led. God is awesome! This is the simplest way to describe the manifested power of God while I used my Ph.D.

At the lifting of the anointing which rested on me, I handed the microphone to the moderator and took my seat. You will never believe what happened next. The fever came right back! "Seriously devil?" I thought. However, God was already glorified; the devil remains horrified and God's people were already edified. Mantled with dunamis, I am unstoppable! God's will being accomplished is what matters.

Once, I visited the dentist and met some men whom I needed to tell about Jesus. We started the conversation until it was my turn to see the dentist. By then the conversation had reached a pinnacle. While getting out of the dentist's chair, he advised that I kept my mouth shut to avoid bleeding.

God knows, I tried! But that which was inside my belly burned so intensely that I soon forgot about the doctor's order. I walked back into the company of men and resumed the declaration of the good news. The men realizing that I was experiencing a little difficulty in speaking, reminded me that I was not supposed to be talking. They promised to avail themselves for the conversation to continue at a more convenient time.

I tell you more, the weather condition does not deter me; I preach rain or shine. The crowd does not impress me; I preach to many or few. Location does not limit me; I preach in the church, the tent, the byways, the hedges; at home and abroad.

One's academic accomplishments do not intimidate me; I preach to the learnt and the unlearnt. Financial remuneration does not appeal to me; freely I have received this gospel, freely I give it. I put it this way, 'Man neva hire mi, suh man caan fire mi' – put another way, I was never hired by man and cannot be fired by man! Glory to God!

I can relate to the prophet Jeremiah's tale of being ostracized and abused for his prophetic utterances by Pashur the priest. Remember him? He was also governor in the house of the LORD. In the account presented in Jeremiah 20, Pashur smote Jeremiah and placed him in stocks - an instrument of punishment. The following day, Jeremiah was released from the stocks by Pashur and immediately the prophet began to speak 'Thus saith the LORD'.

As Jeremiah left prophesying, he began lamenting before God because he was mocked by everyone. Daily, ridicule was his woeful tale and the word of the Lord was made a reproach to him. He decided in verse 9:

> ### *I will not make mention of Him, nor speak any more in His name.*

Similarly, I too have been dealt many hard blows from within and without the body of Christ. Nonetheless, I know that I have been called, anointed and appointed to preach and preach I must! Jeremiah continued to report his experience when he tried to shut his mouth:

> ### *But His word was in mine heart as a burning fire shut up in my bones, and I was weary with forbearing, and I could not stay.*

My God! You see, Jeremiah had not received the baptism with the Holy Ghost and fire. What he was experiencing was periodic anointing, coming upon him to prophesy.

My God from Zion! Well, if that anointing was so powerful that Jeremiah could not keep His mouth closed in the face of insult, abuse, degradation, imprisonment, beatings and other forms of persecution; How can I possibly keep silent when I was born of the water, of the Holy Ghost and of Fire?

Jeremiah felt like fire; but I have got fire in me, on me and around me! Hallelujah to God! I am ablaze for Jesus Christ! His fire within me continually burns out my sins and carnal weaknesses. Simultaneously, His fire on me burns unclean spirits which have been assigned to keep God's people in sin, sickness, bondage and poverty.

I fear nothing and no one when it comes to warring unclean spirits! Reminiscing on my life arouses in me not just a passion to see others saved, delivered, healed and blessed. I know my calling! God called me to deliver those who are oppressed. Oh, my Lord! I am consumed with righteous indignation to see the body of Christ get out of religion and into the Kingdom of Almighty God.

It is time for a shift from the 'exousia' to the 'dunamis'. This is a precursor to being able to see the fulfilment of the prayer we have ritualized:

Thy kingdom come. Thy will be done in earth as it is in heaven (Matthew 6:10).

'Exousia' is a Greek word meaning 'authority' or 'power'. Several scriptures refer to this kind of power. Here are some you can read to establish a clearer understanding of its meaning:

Matthew 7 vs 28-29	**9** v 6	**21** vs 23–27
Ephesians 1 vs 18–23	**2** v 2	**3** vs 10-11
Colossians 1 v 13–20	**2** v 15	
Mark 6 v 7		
Luke 4 v 6		
1 Corinthians 15 vs 20–28		
2 Corinthians 10 v 8		
Romans 9 v 21	**13** vs 1-14	
2 Corinthians 13 v 10		

The Greek word 'dunamis' which appears one hundred and twenty times in the New Testament means 'strength', 'power', or 'ability'. This is where we get the words dynamite and dynamic from.

Here are scripture references of its use for further information:

Mark 9 v 1	Mark 5 v 30	Luke 5 v 17
Luke 9 v 1	Acts 8 v 13	Matthew 22 v 29
Matthew 24 v 30	Luke 1 v 35	Luke 4 v 36
Romans 1 v 20	Hebrews 1 v 3	2 Timothy 1:7
2 Peter 1 v 3	Ephesians 3 v 20–21	2 Corinthians 4 v 7
1 Corinthians 1 v 22–24		
2 Corinthians 12 v 9		

Believers, if we are to truly experience the life Jesus died for us to have, we must move from the flesh realm into the Spirit realm. We need to move beyond the natural into the supernatural. You should realize by now that God cannot be studied, He can only be revealed. The revelation of who God is, comes through relationship and not religion. This will be realized as we are endued with the dunamis power Jesus promised in Acts 1: 4-5,8:

And being assembled together with them commanded them that they should not depart from Jerusalem, but wait for the promise of the Father, which, saith He, ye have heard of Me.

For John truly baptized with water; but ye shall be baptized with the Holy Ghost not many days hence.

But ye shall receive power, after that the Holy Ghost is come upon you: and ye shall be witnesses unto Me both in Jerusalem, and in all Judaea, and in Samaria, and unto the uttermost part of the earth.

The Apostle Paul, a recipient of this dunamis power, prayed in earnest for the believers to receive same in Ephesians 1:17-20

That the God of our Lord Jesus Christ, the Father of glory may give unto you the spirit of wisdom and revelation in the knowledge of Him:

The eyes of your understanding being enlightened; that ye may know what is the hope of His calling, and what the riches of the glory of His inheritance in the saints,

And what is the exceeding greatness of His power to us-ward who believe, according to the working of His mighty power,

Which He wrought in Christ, when He raised Him from the dead and set Him at His own right hand in heavenly places.

In a few years, people will say that they are not worshipping at King Jesus Pentecostal Fellowship in Sheffield, Westmoreland. They will describe everyone in attendance as millionaires and billionaires. This is going to be one of the most common excuses on the lips of our despisers. Yes! We will be millionaires and billionaires, but guess what? They never knew us when we had nothing!

King Jesus Pentecostal Fellowship shall be the first mega-church in western Jamaica! This is a public declaration!

This is a prophetic utterance:

> **King Jesus Pentecostal Fellowship will be the first church in Jamaica, where the dead will be raised after being taken from the morgue. This miracle will be witnessed globally! People are going to remove the bodies of their loved ones from the morgues and bring them to this church, in faith that God is going to bring them back to life.** Hallelujah!

Yeah, I know that some of you are stiff after that declaration. But know this! Your unbelief cannot hinder God from being who He is. Jesus said, ***"I am the resurrection and the life."*** The God whom we have witnessed healing cancer, HIV/AIDS, hypertension, glaucoma, diabetes and all other manner of sicknesses and diseases, is the same God who raises the dead.

It is time to mash down hell! Know that many of you are in your present situation as a result of the demons that have been assigned to you. Unclean spirits have been assigned to ensure that you remain unsuccessful. You can never be wealthy unless you first deal with the demon of poverty which holds you hostage.

God has directed many to the ministry so they can learn how to deal with that situation. In the previous chapter, I gave you the key. The first move is to sow a seed according to the Holy Spirit's direction. Having done that, it is time to command these unclean spirits to take up their weapons and flee!

I HOPE YOU ARE READY TO DO JUST THAT!

If you are, it is time to open your mouth to make declarations over your life. You must be willing to open your mouth, praise God and speak boldly to your situation. There is a dumb demon that holds many people captive. He must be overcome so you can decree and declare, "Thus saith God," over your lives. Watch God transform your mess into a message in response to your obedience.

Listen to me! This dumb spirit is very active among many Apostolics too. He is at work in those who nod their heads and merely wave their hands whenever it is time to get radical and give God the praise He deserves. Open your mouth! God is a speaking Spirit and if you belong to Him, you are too.

Chains are broken, captives are set free, healing, deliverance, and breakthroughs are all possible in the midst of praise and worship. Come on now worshippers, all who are believing God for miraculous breakthroughs. Open your mouth! It is time to worship your way to victory! Hallelujah!

It's time for you to break out in praise and worship. Hallelujah! No more bowing of the head! Get out of that mentality! The time for worship is not a time for bowing of the head but rather a time to open your mouth and praise the Lord.

Praise the Lord!

Praise the Lord!

Open your mouth and say something!

Are you a true worshipper?

It is time to kick the devil out of your life now!

I say that it is time to kick the devil out of your life now!

Are you ready? If you are, then this next segment is yours. Hallelujah! This is how the enemy works. Satan and his unclean spirits are not omnipresent; they function in time. Therefore, they assign a particular number of demons to fight your life for a specific period. At the expiration of this assignment, a new set of unclean spirits are assigned to your life for another season.

In the case of witchcraft, what people do is to pay money for the witchcraft workers to assign unclean spirits to your life. These demons are instructed to perform specific destructive tasks which hinder your success. A curse can therefore block your prosperity until the period for which the payment was received expires. That could be days, weeks, months or even years.

There are also unclean spirits assigned to us through the involvement of our fore parents in witchcraft or other forms of evil. In such cases, the curse is passed down from three or four generations. Now that is a great dilemma! But bless God, there is a solution! It is in your mouth! You must open your mouth and break the curse. Let the devil know that the curse stops here.

There could be a cancer demon in your family and as a result of that, your grandmother died from cancer. The demon moves down to the next generation and claims the life of an aunt. Not long after, another family member dies also from cancer. Why? Because no one in the family has dared to open their mouth. What are you going to do about it? You definitely have a choice! Get radical and slap that devil in the face and declare, "IT STOPS HERE!"

Do not let anyone tell you that it is hereditary. Slap that devil! Don't let anyone tell you that diabetes runs in the family. Slap that devil! Command him to get out of your life and out of your family.

There are unclean spirits in your life that are fighting you. I remember once, the Lord spoke to me about the importance of being cautious about the places I visit. He taught me that I can experience demonic attacks from visiting certain places where unclean spirits are lingering. The warning was to ensure that without the direction of the Spirit of God, I do not enter these territories.

As believers in Christ, we are admonished to:

> *Be sober, be vigilant; because your adversary the devil; as a roaring lion, walketh about, seeking whom he may devour*
> *1 Peter 5:8.*

Unexplained disasters could begin to manifest in your life after being in environments where the Lord did not send you. A common saying in Jamaica is, "mi nuh kno wah happen, all of a sudden mi jus salt."

Another means of demonic transference is through intimate relationships. Many people get involved sexually with partners whose lifestyle led to them becoming hosts to hundreds of unclean spirits. Unaware, these unclean spirits are transferred from one partner to the next. The life of the individual which the unclean spirits enter begins to be characterized by chaos and anarchy.

The affected partner begins to question the origin of all these strange occurrences. All is traced back to the commencement of this relationship. They were released through intimate encounters. Success then begins to elude the once successful partner, and failure sets in.

There are occasions where these unclean spirits continue to operate in an individual's life, long after the relationship is terminated. A man possessing a demon of violence could release this demon in the life of a sex partner before leaving the relationship. This individual then continues to experience violence in every successive relationship.

A woman could enter a relationship and later discover that the man is married. She immediately ends the relationship and later enters another relationship. Guess what? She discovers that this person is also married! Why? It is a demon attacking her life!

Enough said, any situation that hinders us from becoming what God intended us to become, requires warfare. Anything that blocks us from having whatever God intended for us to have, calls for war. Whatever deters us from doing what God intended for us to do, must be warred. If we are unable to go wherever God intended for us to go, it is time to declare WAR!

That is my mandate! As God reveals the strategies that the enemy employs to defeat God's people, I release them. As He reveals the methods to be utilized to overcome the devil, I employ them. They will be utilized with full force in spiritual warfare until God's people are delivered from bondage. No retreat! No surrender!

It is my bound duty to fight for myself and my family. But I am just as committed to the task of fighting for my loved ones and fellow men. That includes you! I am determined to see everyone I encounter, live the abundant life Jesus died for us to have. I am a warrior! I war unclean spirits and lead God's people to engage the enemy in warfare as well.

Knowledge is power! Wisdom is the principal thing! And with all thy getting, get understanding. Revelations from the Holy Spirit are to be enacted so that we can defeat the enemy and live a victorious life. This calls for WAR!!!

In my first book -Warring Unclean Spirits- much valuable information, testimonies and instructions are available for all who desire the victorious life in Christ. That tool, along with this, will make you a force to be reckoned with by the kingdom of darkness. As the Holy Ghost empowers you, defeat will be a thing of the past. From this moment forward you will successfully engage the enemy in spiritual warfare.

IT IS TIME FOR WAR!!!!

We are now going to speak to every month of the year: January, February, March, April, May, June, July, August, September, October, November and December. We speak to every month of the year and every demon assigned to these months too.

Yes! I know this is mind-blowing and deep. Regardless, as God leads, I release these revelations to empower His people with information and strategies. Without strategies, we will be defeated. Our enemy, Satan is regimented and very strategic in his operations. We too, need to be strategic, united, equipped and organized.

Why do you think persons born within the same month, display similar behaviour? Why do people generally ask, "Which month were you born?" This information is meant to determine the behaviour that should characterize an individual based on their birth month.

Statements like these are common: January people are kind; February people are jovial; we are ruled under the same sign. Some are not very receptive to this message because of their present addictions to horoscopes. Nonetheless, I am still required to tell you the truth. These practices are unacceptable to God! They are controlled by unclean spirits and are demonic.

The behaviours of the children of God are not dictated and influenced by zodiac signs but by the Holy Ghost which indwells the believer. In the Kingdom of God, we are not ruled under signs but under the power of God. We have power over the signs! Is there anyone who understands what I am talking about?

There are demons attached to every month and the origin of the names of the months speaks volumes:

January from a god named Janus
February from a festival called Februa
March from Mars
April from goddess Aphrodite
May from the goddess Maia
June from the queen of gods Juno

July from Julius Caesar
August from Augustus Caesar
September from septem, the Latin word for seven
October from octo, the Latin word for eight
November from Novem, the Latin word for nine
December from decem, the Latin word for ten

I imagine that some readers are now beginning to see me as strange. However, I am telling you the truth and we are going to deal with these devils right now in the name of Jesus. Come on warriors! I need the praisers and true worshippers to come in agreement with me and declare that we are controlled by the Holy Spirit and will not participate in horoscope readings.

Open your mouth and declare war! Come on! Declare war! Hear me; the church is controlled by the Spirit of God! The church carries power over every seasonal spirit. The plagues affecting the world will not affect the people of God. Just as it was in Egypt when the flies and frogs were affecting the Egyptians, so shall it be with us. Although there were no walls to separate the Israelites from their enemies, not one frog or fly entered Goshen, where the people of God dwelt.

Yes! The flies and frogs could never pass over into Goshen to plague the children of God! Likewise, no demon should be defeating us, as God's people. Our dwelling is our Goshen. This house of worship is our Goshen. There is a war raging, but whenever the enemy comes in like a flood, the Spirit of the Lord lifts up a standard against him Isaiah 59:19.

Today, the Spirit of God lifts up a standard against cancer! The Spirit of God lifts up a standard against diabetes! Open your mouth and declare war! Hear me! I say that you need to declare war against these monthly demons. These demons can be assigned against you and every year you discover that there is a new assignment against your life. Reassessing your past, you conclude that you were being blocked from prospering every year.

Rest assured that through the power of the Holy Ghost, you carry an anointing that is effective from January to December. Regardless of what is set for the child of God to fail, this anointing goes before us. It is like a pillar of fire by night and a pillar of cloud by day. It burns unclean spirits! In other words, as the enemies confront us, the Holy Ghost shall consume them.

There will be some devils coming behind us that we cannot see, but the word of God declares in Psalm 91:

> *He that dwelleth in the secret place of the Most High shall abide under the shadow of the Almighty.*

Hallelujah! Declare it! Come on! Open your mouth!
I am covered!
Let the devil know, "I am covered!"

Open your mouth and let the devil know, I am covered! I fear no duppy (ghost).

Psalm 37 v 1-2:

> *Fret not thyself because of evildoers, neither be thou envious against the workers of iniquity.*
>
> *For they shall soon be cut down like the grass, and wither as the green herb.*

Psalm 121 v 1-2:

> *I will lift mine eyes unto the hills, from whence cometh my help.*
>
> *My help cometh from the LORD, which made heaven and earth.*

Where does your help come from? Well, mine comes from the LORD who made heaven and earth. Hallelujah!

Help is on the way!

Breakthrough is on the way!

It is time to push back some dark clouds! God is going to push back the enemy! This is the year that God is going to bless your mess and give you a message. This year God is going to turn it around!

What was your weakness shall become your strength. Come on believers, we are warring some demons now. All that God requires of you is to worship. Whenever you worship, the Lord your God shall go before you and make your path straight.

Come on now! Wherever you are, raise your hands in the air. This moment is for partakers in the glory of God and not for those who just desire to see God manifesting through others. Right where you are at this very moment;

You are at the right place; at the right time for your miracle!

You are at the right place; at the right time for your breakthrough.

It is up to you!

Use your worship to prepare the atmosphere for the Shekinah Glory of God to show up. Our God inhabits the praises of His people. Wherever God shows up, deliverance, salvation, miracles, breakthroughs, infilling with the Holy Ghost and fire baptism are inevitable. Come on! Prepare the way for the King of Glory to enter your messy situation. It will be transformed into a beautiful message right now.

You did not just desire to read this book because you are curious to get the juicy details of my past. I believe you are reading because you desire the blessings of God to overtake you. Surely, it is not your intention to be clogged up with gossip, heresies and fables. Instead, that desire to be blessed shall be met as you praise God for it.

It is time to forget those things which are behind us and PRESS! It is time to go forward! The devil has held you down way too long. You have been incapacitated for a very, very, very, long time! God says that this is the year for your mighty breakthrough. We are taking it in the name of Jesus! And we are taking it by force!

Are you ready to take it? Let me ask again! Are you ready to take it? Listen to me and listen good - just as the enemy strategically plans what he is going to unleash against your life each month of the year; I want you to know that God has a plan to do good in your life, every month of the year.

I want you to release twelve praises to God. One for each month of the year, then watch as every demon which has been assigned against you for any month of the year, aborts his plan, in the name of Jesus.

When you release this praise, the Holy Ghost shall push it back in the name of Jesus. The fire of God shall roast every unclean spirit assigned to hinder this season of breakthrough in your life in Jesus' name.

Open your mouth and give God twelve shouts of praise! Believe that every curse is broken right now! Watch out! For every blessing coming your way is being released with an unstoppable force!

Hallelujah! I feel something! Hallelujah! I feel something that the enemy has been blocking is about to be released right now in Jesus' name! Like Daniel, the prince demon blocking your answer from the Lord has been holding up the angel. You have been fasting and seeking God in earnest.

God says that it is your time!

Your season!

Your day!

HAPPY NEW YEAR!!!!

No devil in hell can stop this one!

Hallelujah! Give Him praise and glory right here!

Hallelujah!

Frankly, I do not care which month of the year you are in right now. I believe that God has a retroactive blessing to release to His people. If any month has already passed in the year, believe God that these twelve praises will release whatever the enemy hindered you from receiving in any previous month.

Hallelujah! I told you it is wartime! YES! We are warring for our blessings! We are warring for our breakthroughs! My God! That is how mighty our God is and you know what? We are demanding payment with interest!

If you believe it, you can receive it in Jesus' name! People of God, you should know:

> *We wrestle not against flesh and blood, but against principalities, against powers, against the rulers of the darkness of this world, against spiritual wickedness in high places Ephesians 6:12.*

So then, the battle is first won in the spirit. I repeat, the battle is first won in the spirit. I found it necessary to reinforce that. That is the way it is with a wealthy person.

They knew they would be wealthy in their minds before their wealth materialized physically.

I wonder if you understand what I am saying to you. If you were to give Twenty million dollars to an individual who has not won the battle over poverty mentality, within five years, that individual would be broke again.

Shocked? You need not be! Just look at the persons with a pauper's mentality who wins the lottery. Even if the winning is as big as Forty million dollars, they will still be a pauper in another five years.

Ever wondered why? Listen, his mind was not prepared for the money he received. Tell yourself and anyone around you, "Win the battle in your mind first! Win the battle in your mind first! Win the battle in your mind first!"

Envision yourself opening your own door with your own key. See yourself owning your own business. You must first take it, in the spiritual realm and the manifestation will occur in the physical realm. Do you understand now?

We will not procrastinate in spiritual warfare either. The demons which have been assigned to affect you next week, next month or even next year are going to be dealt with right now in the name of Jesus! Declare it loudly and clearly, "I am dealing with the demons which have assigned themselves against me today!"

For some persons, the demons have been assigned to ensure that you do not remain in the church. Let that devil know that you are sending up praises now, for even the years to come. Praise God in advance! For you shall not backslide!

Are you ready for war? We are coming against the demons assigned to attack you in January with a praise. This praise shall pull down the glory of God and it shall defeat all those spirits and push them back. Get ready to release a praise for:

JANUARY!!!!!!!!!!!!
    SHOOOOOOOUT!!!!!!!!!!!!!
FEBRUARY!!!!!!!!!!!!!
    SHOOOOOOOUT!!!!!!!!!!!!!
MARCH!!!!!!!!!!!!!!
    SHOOOOOOOUT!!!!!!!!!!!!!
APRIL!!!!!!!!!!!!!!
    SHOOOOOOOUT!!!!!!!!!!!!!
MAY!!!!!!!!!!!!!!
    SHOOOOOOOUT!!!!!!!!!!!!
JUNE!!!!!!!!!!!!!!
    SHOOOOOOOOUT!!!!!!!!!!!!!
JULY!!!!!!!!!!!!!!
    SHOOOOOOOOUT!!!!!!!!!!!!!
AUGUST!!!!!!!!!!!!!!
    SHOOOOOOOUT!!!!!!!!!!!!!!
SEPTEMBER!!!!!!!!!!!!!!
    SHOOOOOOOUT!!!!!!!!!!!!!!

OCTOBER!!!!!!!!!!!!
       SHOOOOOOOUT!!!!!!!!!!!!!
NOVEMBER!!!!!!!!!!!!
       SHOOOOOOOUT!!!!!!!!!!!!!
DECEMBER!!!!!!!!!!!!
       SHOOOOOOOUT!!!!!!!!!!!!!

Take your job!

Take strength!

Take back your anointing!

I say, take back your anointing!

Take it by force!

Take back your gift!

I say, take back your gift!

Take it by force!

Open your mouth and speak to your situation! Open your mouth and speak over your life in Jesus' name!

Fresh anointing! Fresh anointing! Hallelujah!

Holy Ghost! Holy Ghost! Holy Ghost! Hallelujah!

Yes! Holy Ghost!

Take your healing, both for yourself and your children!

Take back your daughters!

Take back your sons! Let the devil know that they belong to God.

If you need the infilling of the Holy Ghost, take it! The Holy Ghost is already given so take it by force today! Hallelujah!

Come on worshippers! I am not the least bit concerned about the type of pressure you are undergoing. That's not important. Declare that this is the year of your deliverance! Take it with your praise! Hallelujah! All those who are held in bondage by unclean spirits today, praise your way out!

God says that you are free! You are loosed! They will NOT continue to affect your life after today in Jesus' name!

Jesus! Jesus! Jesus! Go ahead and praise Him right now! Hallelujah! He is Lord! Hallelujah! Get in the Holy Ghost and praise Him! Holy Ghost! Holy Ghost! Jesus!

If you have not yet surrendered your life to Jesus Christ, it is your time now! Hallelujah! It is your time to surrender and be baptized in the name of Jesus. Yes! Listen to me, somewhere the water is troubled and God is saying, **"Today is the day of recreation for you."** He wants to recreate you into a new being. He wants to redeem, renew, revive and restore you today. Today God says, **"I am doing a new thing in you."**

I encourage you to find a church and get baptized in Jesus' name today. The water is troubled! It is your time now! Come into a new life as you take on the name of Jesus Christ!

COME! COME! COME!

It is your time to be baptized in the name of Jesus Christ. You promised the Lord that if He just did that one thing for you, you were going to serve Him. He answered your cry, now it is your turn to keep your end of the bargain. Come!

Jesus says that this is a new day; a new beginning for you. Come! Allow God to do for you what He did for me. Come!

He took me from condemnation to consecration.

He took me from the pit and placed me in the pulpit.

He took my mess and gave me the message that I am now giving you.

He took me from the 'guttermost' and placed me in the uttermost.

I have given you the key to enter the Kingdom of God. It is accepting Jesus Christ as your Lord and Saviour.

Now the choice to come to the next level is yours. Are you ready?

If your answer is "YES!"

Welcome kingdom citizens!

Welcome to the uttermost, royal heirs of the Kingdom of God!

Printed in the USA
CPSIA information can be obtained
at www.ICGtesting.com
CBHW030449221123
2029CB00002B/2